Programmed Ear Training

Second Edition

Volume I:

Intervals; Melody and Rhythm

Leo Horacek
Professor Emeritus
West Virginia University

Gerald Lefkoff
West Virginia University

HBJ

Harcourt Brace Jovanovich, Publishers
San Diego New York Chicago Austin Washington, D.C.
London Sydney Tokyo Toronto

ISBN: 0-15-572026-0
Library of Congress Catalog Card Number: 88-81050
Printed in the United States of America

Programmed Ear Training
Second Edition

Volume I:
Intervals; Melody and Rhythm

CONTENTS

LESSON CASSETTES VOLUME 1

Cassette 1
Side A A1-1, A1-2, A1-3, A1-4
Side B A1-5, A1-6, A1-7, A1-8

Cassette 2
Side A A1-9, A1-10, A1-11, A1-12
Side B A2-1, A2-2, A2-3, A2-4

Cassette 3
Side A A2-5, A2-6, A2-7 A2-8
Side B A2-9, A3-1, A3-2, A3-3

Cassette 4
Side A A3-4, A3-5, A3-6, A3-7
Side B A3-8, A3-9, A4-1, A4-2

Cassette 5
Side A A4-3, A4-4, A4-5, A4-6
Side B A4-7, A5-1, A5-2, A5-3

Cassette 6
Side A A5-4, A5-5, A5-6, A5-7
Side B A5-8, A5-9, A5-10, A5-11

Cassette 7
Side A A6-1, A6-2, A6-3, A6-4
Side B A6-5, A6-6, A6-7, A7-1

Cassette 8
Side A A7-2, A7-3, A7-4, A7-5
Side B A7-6, A7-7, A7-8

Cassette 9
Side A B1-1, B1-2, B1-3, B1-4
Side B B2-1, B2-2, B2-3, B2-4

Cassette 10
Side A B2-5, B2-6, B2-7, B3-1
Side B B3-2, B3-3, B3-4, B4-1

Cassette 11
Side A B4-2, B4-3, B4-4, B5-1
Side B B5-2, B5-3, B5-4, B5-5

Cassette 12
Side A B5-6, B5-7, B5-8, B6-1
Side B B6-2, B6-3, B6-4, B7-1

Cassette 13
Side A B7-2, B7-3, B8-1, B8-2
Side B B8-3, B8-4, B8-5, B9-1

Cassette 14
Side A B9-2, B9-3, B9-4, B9-5
Side B B10-1, B10-2, B10-3, B11-1

Cassette 15
Side A B11-2, B11-3, B12-1, B12-2
Side B B12-3, B13-1, B13-2, B13-3

Cassette 16
Side A B13-4, B13-5, B13-6, B13-7
Side B B13-8, B13-9, B14-1, B14-2

Cassette 17
Side A B14-3, B14-4, B14-5, B14-6
Side B B15-1, B15-2, B15-3, B16-1

Cassette 18
Side A B16-2, B16-3, B16-4, B16-5
Side B B17-1, B17-2, B17-3

LESSON CASSETTES VOLUME II

Cassette 19
Side A C1-1, C1-2, C1-3, C1-4
Side B C1-5, C1-6, C1-7, C2-1

Cassette 20
Side A C2-2, C2-3, C2-4, C3-1
Side B C3-2, C3-3, C3-4, C4-1

Cassette 21
Side A C4-2, C4-3, C5-1, C5-2
Side B C5-3, C5-4, C6-1, C6-2

Cassette 22
Side A C6-3, C6-4, C7-1, C7-2
Side B C7-3, C7-4, C8-1, C8-2

Cassette 23
Side A C8-3, C8-4, C8-5
Side B C8-6, C8-7

Cassette 24
Side A C9-1, C9-2, C9-3
Side B C9-4, C9-5, C9-6

Cassette 25
Side A D1-1, D1-2, D1-3, D2-1
Side B D2-2, D3-1, D3-2, D3-3

Cassette 26
Side A D4-1, D4-2, D4-3, D4-4
Side B D5-1, D5-2, D5-3, D5-4

Cassette 27
Side A D5-5, D5-6, D6-1, D6-2
Side B D6-3, D6-4, D7-1, D7-2

Cassette 28
Side A D7-3, D7-4, D8-1, D8-2
Side B D8-3, D8-4, D8-5, D8-6

Cassette 29
Side A D9-1, D9-2, D10-1, D10-2
Side B D10-3, D10-4, D10-5, D11-1

Cassette 30
Side A D11-2, D11-3, D11-4
Side B D12-1, D12-2

Cassette 31
Side A D12-3, D12-4, D12-5
Side B D13-1, D13-2

TEST CASSETTES VOLUMES I and II

Test Cassette 1
Side A A2a, A2b, A3a, A3b
Side B A4, A6, A7

Test Cassette 2
Side A B1, B2, B3, B4
Side B B5, B6, B7, B8

Test Cassette 3
Side A B9, B10
Side B B11, B12

Test Cassette 4
Side A B13, B14, B15
Side B B16, B17

Test Cassette 5
Side A C1, C2, C3
Side B C4, C5, C6

Test Cassette 6
Side A C7a, C7b, C7c
Side B C7d, C8, C9

Test Cassette 7
Side A D1, D2, D3
Side B D4, D5

Test Cassette 8
Side A D6, D7a, D7b
Side B D7c, D7d, D8

Test Cassette 9
Side A D9, D10, D11
Side B D12, D13

INTRODUCTION

Programmed Ear Training was designed to fit the goals of the ear-training portion of typical freshman and sophomore theory programs. The flexible organization permits it to be used in a number of ways.

1. It will fit an ear-training course that combines class and individualized instruction.
2. It can provide a completely independent self-instruction course.
3. It can be used to provide a supplement to class instruction for enrichment or remedial purposes.
4. It can be used for independent preparation for special tests such as entrance or qualifying examinations.

The skills and understandings called "ear-training" consist primarily of the establishment of mental relationships between sounds and symbols. The sounds are musical tones, melodies, rhythms, and chords. The symbols form musical notation or designate intervals or chords.

The great variety, number, and complexity in these sounds and symbols requires a large number of separate presentations for substantial learning. It is usually difficult to provide a sufficient amount of this experience for each student in a class situation. Because of this, *Programmed Ear Training* was designed to give thousands of separate sound and symbol presentations, covering most of the types of melodic, rhythmic, and chordal patterns commonly found in music, in a system that is economical with both student and teacher time.

Programmed instruction can have two important advantages, both of which are found in *Programmed Ear Training*. First, most of the work can be done with little or no help from a teacher. Second, because programmed instruction can be very flexible, the student can progress at his own rate, moving rapidly where the work is easy and more slowly where it is difficult.

A basic procedure for programmed instruction, used in most of the lessons in this book, is as follows: The material to be learned is broken into segments, often small, sometimes longer, in each of which the student is presented with a problem and asked to make a response. Immediately after the response, the student is provided with the correct answer. Through many confirmations of correct responses and corrections of incorrect responses, complicated and difficult skills and concepts can be learned.

The skills developed through this course of study can be valuable in almost any musical activity. Not only are they important in musical performance, but they also can help in the understanding of music as it is heard, in arranging and writing music, in musical discussion, and in learning about music of various styles and periods.

ORGANIZATION

Programmed Ear Training consists of two student volumes and a set of cassette tape recordings. The content of the student volumes is divided into four parts. In the first volume are found Part A, *Intervals*, and Part B, *Melody and Rhythm*. In the second volume are Part C, *Introductory Harmony*, and Part D, *Advanced Harmony*.

Various sequences of working through the parts of these volumes are possible. Parts A, B, and C are independent and need not be begun in that order. Part D, however, being advanced harmony, should be started only after completion of Part C.

Each of the four parts is divided into *series*, each dealing with a different musical content or skill, and each series is made up of *lessons*. Within the parts, different sequences are possible in the use of the series. These alternate sequences are suggested in the introduction to each part.

For every lesson, there is a tape recording to provide the sounds of the intervals, melodies, or chords for that lesson. Nearly all the lessons also make use of printed materials. In some cases in Parts C and D, a given tape recording is used for several lessons.

With most lessons, a label designates both the printed page and the tape for that lesson. For example, A3-2 indicates both the worksheets and the tape recording for a lesson. The *A* indicates that it is in Part A; the number 3, just after the *A*, shows that it is the third series in Part A; and the number 2, after the dash, shows that it is the second lesson in its series. Where several lessons make use of the same tape, a letter is added to the label on the printed page. For example, C1-4a, C1-4b, and C1-4c are three lessons using tape C1-4.

With some series, lesson supplements contain printed material for which there is no tape recording. These are primarily for additional sightsinging and dictation in class. The sightsinging supplements are found in the student volumes. The dictation materials appear in the *Instructor's Manual*, which the instructor should have.

Most of the lessons are intended for repeated study, and indeed were especially designed to be beneficially repeated for increased skill. Thus, multiple copies of the worksheets are included for those lessons requiring written responses: usually three copies of full-page answer sheets and four copies of half-page sheets.

TIPS ON STUDYING

Here are some suggestions for making your study more effective.

Lessons with Short Items

Many of the lessons make use of short items of rhythm, melody, or chords, and may involve sightsinging, dictation, or identification. The following suggestions apply to these lessons.

1. Do not listen to the tapes without making responses. The most effective learning occurs when the learner makes definite responses.
2. Make responses quickly without stopping to analyze. Immediately check your answer for correctness and go directly to the next item. Wide experience with numerous varied patterns is essential in ear training. Analysis is generally less important.
3. Do not be unduly bothered by errors you may make. Errors are an almost necessary part of discrimination learning. Ultimately, you should learn to make right responses in a large proportion of the items, but errors should always be expected, especially in early stages.

4. Do not dally between items. Very often, one item is a prompt or reference for the next item. In lessons involving singing, you should usually proceed in tempo without stopping the tape. Where time is needed to write an answer, stop the tape only long enough to respond.

Lessons with Long Passages for Dictation

The following suggestions apply to dictation of long items where repeated hearings may be involved.

5. Memorize what you hear before beginning to write. Listen as many times as necessary for this. Think through what you have heard either in your imagination or by singing to yourself. Once the sound is memorized, you can manipulate it in your mind—going back and forth, starting and stopping, and changing the tempo—as you figure out the notation or symbols required.
6. On repeated hearings of an item, it may be useful to focus one time on pitch, the next time on rhythm, another time on the bass line, another on the soprano, or on the chord-types, etc.
7. When you check your response, do not be overly disturbed by errors. First focus on what was done correctly, then move on and concentrate on the other aspects in the following items.

Lessons with Long Passages for Sightsinging

Where long melodies are used for reading at first sight, which is the ultimate goal, no particular suggestions are necessary. However, sometimes long melodies are used for prepared sightsinging. For these, the following suggestions are offered.

8. Work at the piano, but use it primarily to verify what you have sung, not for rote study. In preparing for performance, it can be helpful to practice certain parts or aspects separately, for example, difficult portions, connection of parts, pitches alone, rhythm alone, or recitation of solmization. After this, the various aspects can be put together with the goal of singing the phrases correctly and fluently without hesitation, with security and ease.

Repetition of Lessons

Most of the lessons are designed to be used a number of times. The following suggestions may help in making decisions about repeating lessons.

9. It can be helpful to repeat a lesson, either immediately or at the next practice session, so long as you feel you are progressing. If you do not seem to be improving, it may be better to move on to other material for the moment. Often further progress can be made in coming back to that lesson at a later time.
10. Sometimes in repeating a lesson, you may obtain fewer right answers than before. This should not be interpreted as "going backwards." Human behavior is always variable, and there is always an element of chance in complex activities. Even if you already have reached a peak in the skills of a given lesson, it can be useful to review them to keep them current. Probably some learning of value always takes place.
11. Reviewing a lesson after some time has passed can help to solidify the competencies involved. It can be especially helpful before a test.
12. An entire series or study unit can be beneficially studied a second time to develop improved competency. This is particularly true after the study of more advanced related materials.

Individual Needs

The best way of working is not the same for every student. The following suggestions may help you decide what is best for you.

13. The length of an individual study session will depend on your attention span. You can study as long as you can concentrate. If your mind wanders, take a short break, or finish what you are doing and stop.
14. Find an optimum length of time to set up for your study sessions—one during which you can concentrate well and that is long enough to cover a substantial amount of material.
15. Experiment to determine which is better for you: frequent short sessions or less frequent longer sessions. Frequent short sessions can be especially beneficial for review and maintaining skills already learned. Long sessions can be beneficial for intensive work on particular learning goals.

SOLMIZATION

In sightsinging, some musicians make extensive use of syllables. The general practice is called *solmization*. Others prefer not to use syllables, sometimes considering them an unhelpful complication. Sometimes even students who want to use syllables have an incomplete knowledge of the system they are using. To help those who want a more complete grasp of the use of syllables, we have presented below a description of some of the more widely used systems of syllables.

Solfeggio

Solfeggio involves the use of the familiar *do-re-mi* syllables. The syllables *do re mi fa sol la ti do* match the ascending major scale in which half-steps are formed by the succession *mi-fa* and *ti-do*. The other adjacent intervals are whole steps. Chromatic alterations can be indicated by a change of the vowel sound. The syllables other than *mi* and *ti* can be raised a half-step by changing the vowel to *i* (pronounced *ee*). With one exception, a half-step lowering is shown by changing the vowel to *e* (pronounced *ay*). The exception is *re*. Lowering of *re* is indicated by the vowel *a* (pronounced *rah*). Thus the ascending chromatic scale is *do di re ri mi fa fi sol si la li ti do*. The descending chromatic scale is *do ti te la le sol se fa mi me re ra do*. Three common ways of using solfeggio are described below.

Key Signature Solfeggio In key signature solfeggio, the syllables match the intervals created by the key signature with *mi-fa* and *ti-do* falling on the half-steps. Thus *do* is the tonic for a major key, and *la* the tonic for a minor key.

Tonic-*do* Solfeggio In tonic-*do* solfeggio, *do* will always match the first degree of the key, the tonic, whether the mode is major or minor. Vowel alteration of syllables will then reflect the pattern of half- and whole-steps found in minor keys. For example, with this system the melodic minor scale is *do re me fa sol la ti do te le sol fa me re do*.

Fixed-*do* Solfeggio In fixed-*do* solfeggio, *do* always indicates *C*-natural, *re* indicates *D*-natural, and so forth.

Note-Name Singing

In note-name singing, the syllables are derived from note-names, each having a letter and an accidental: for example, C-natural, F-sharp, and B-flat. For notes without sharps or flats, the letter alone is used. For convenience, the words sharp and flat can be abbreviated to the first consonant sound, the sharp being indicated by *sh* and the flat by *f*. Thus C-sharp will be pronounced *ceesh*, and B-flat will be pronounced *beef*. Since all the syllables except *F* end in a vowel sound, it will make a nicely consistent system if *F* is pronounced *fee*. Thus the natural notes would be pronounced *aee bee cee dee ee fee gee*. The notes with sharps would be *aeesh, beesh, ceesh, deesh, eesh, feesh, geesh*, and with flats *aeef, beef, ceef, deef, eef, feef, geef, aeef, beef*. For double-sharps, *eesh* is added to the syllable (F-double-sharp becomes *feesheesh*). For double-flats *eef* is added (B-double-flat becomes *beefeef*).

Key-Degree Singing

In key-degree singing, the syllables are derived from the key-degree numbers. To facilitate singing, the pronunciation of some of the numbers can be modified. *Seven* can be reduced to one syllable and pronounced either as *sev* or *seh*. For fast singing, the *v* in *five* and the *x* in *six* can be dropped. Thus the scale degrees in a key would be *one, two, three, four, five* (or *fi*), *six* (or *si*), and *sev* (or *seh*).

PART A

INTERVALS

INTRODUCTION

Part A is concerned with ear-training skills that involve intervals. These skills are discrimination, sightsinging, dictation, and identification. Part A is not prerequisite to Parts B or C. Indeed, the somewhat abstract settings for many of the intervals make much of the work more difficult than the beginnings of Parts B and C. A recommended procedure is to begin Part A concurrently with the beginning of Part B. Study of Part A is particularly useful at two times: 1) in the early study of ear training as an introduction to elemental pitch relations, and 2) after considerable experience with melody and harmony in a tonal setting, with the objective of greater mastery of abstract pitch relationships.

Part A contains seven series, each devoted to a particular skill. The first four series deal with melodic intervals, and the remaining three with harmonic intervals. Series A1, discrimination of single melodic intervals, is intended as a skill preliminary to other melodic interval series. For some students, it may be feasible to omit Series A1 and to begin melodic interval study with Series A2. Series A2, sightsinging, Series A3, dictation, and Series A4, interval identification, are coordinate and can be done in any order.

Series A5, discrimination of single harmonic intervals, is a skill preliminary to other harmonic interval series. As with Series A1, it may be feasible for some students to omit Series A5 and begin harmonic interval study with Series A6. Series A6, dictation, and Series A7, interval identification, are coordinate and can be done in any order.

Two possible plans exist for the sequence of lessons in Part A. The first plan is the sequence found in the book. In the second plan, lessons containing similar intervals are selected from the different series and grouped as study units. A syllabus for this second plan follows.

1. Seconds

A1-1 Melodic interval discrimination: minor seconds
A1-2 Melodic interval discrimination: major seconds
A2-1 Interval sightsinging
A3-1 Melodic interval dictation
A5-1 Harmonic interval discrimination: minor seconds
A5-2 Harmonic interval discrimination: major seconds
A6-1 Harmonic interval dictation
A7-1 Harmonic interval identification

2. Thirds

A1-3 Melodic interval discrimination: minor thirds
A1-4 Melodic interval discrimination: major thirds
A2-2 Interval sightsinging
A3-2 Melodic interval dictation
A4-1 Melodic interval identification
A5-3 Harmonic interval discrimination: minor thirds
A5-4 Harmonic interval discrimination: major thirds
A6-2 Harmonic interval dictation
A7-2 Harmonic interval identification

3. Fourths and Fifths

A1-5 Melodic interval discrimination: perfect fourths
A1-6 Melodic interval discrimination: tritones
A1-7 Melodic interval discrimination: perfect fifths
A2-3 Interval sightsinging
A3-3 Melodic interval dictation
A4-2 Melodic interval identification
A5-5 Harmonic interval discrimination: perfect fourths
A5-6 Harmonic interval discrimination: tritones
A5-7 Harmonic interval discrimination: perfect fifths
A6-3 Harmonic interval dictation
A7-3 Harmonic interval identification

4. Sixths

A1-8 Melodic interval discrimination: minor sixths
A1-9 Melodic interval discrimination: major sixths
A2-4 Interval sightsinging
A3-4 Melodic interval dictation
A4-3 Melodic interval identification
A5-8 Harmonic interval discrimination: minor sixths
A5-9 Harmonic interval discrimination: major sixths
A6-4 Harmonic interval dictation
A7-4 Harmonic interval identification

5. Sevenths and Octaves

A1-10 Melodic interval discrimination: minor sevenths
A1-11 Melodic interval discrimination: major sevenths
A2-5 Interval sightsinging
A3-5 Melodic interval dictation
A4-4 Melodic interval identification
A5-10 Harmonic interval discrimination: minor sevenths
A5-11 Harmonic interval discrimination: major sevenths
A6-5 Harmonic interval dictation
A7-5 Harmonic interval identification

6. All Intervals Together

A2-6 Interval sightsinging: treble clef
A2-8 Interval sightsinging: bass clef
A3-6 Melodic interval dictation: treble clef
A3-8 Melodic interval dictation: bass clef
A4-5 Melodic interval identification

A4-6 Melodic interval identification
A7-6 Harmonic interval identification: thirds and sixths
A7-7 Harmonic interval identification: seconds, sevenths, and tritones
A6-6 Harmonic interval dictation
A2-7 Interval sightsinging: treble clef
A2-9 Interval sightsinging: bass clef
A3-7 Melodic interval dictation: treble clef
A3-9 Melodic interval dictation: bass clef
A4-7 Melodic interval identification
A6-7 Harmonic interval dictation
A7-8 Harmonic interval identification: all intervals

SERIES A1

MELODIC INTERVAL DISCRIMINATION

The purpose of this series is to develop the ability to discriminate between melodic intervals when they are heard.

The pitch difference between two tones is called an *interval.* If the two tones are played together, the interval is called *harmonic*. If the two tones occur one after the other, the interval is called *melodic*. It is important for the music student to learn to tell the difference between sizes of intervals.

Each lesson in this series is devoted to a particular interval. The purpose is not to name that interval, but only to discriminate it from intervals of other sizes. There is a tape recording for each lesson, but no worksheet. Scrap paper can be used for answers.

On the tape, you will hear a variety of intervals. The task is to recognize the particular interval to which the lesson is devoted, and to respond by making a mark on the paper. You do not need to indicate the name of the interval, but only to recognize the sound of it. For example, the first lesson is devoted to the interval of the minor second—that is, two tones a half-step apart. This interval is mixed in with other intervals. Sometimes the intervals will be high, sometimes low or in the middle register. But whenever you think you hear an interval that is a minor second, you should make a tally mark on the paper. After each minor second on this tape, following a brief pause, a high electronic tone will be heard. If the electronic tone is heard after you make a tally mark, you will know the response was correct. If you have made a mark and failed to hear the tone, you will know you made an error. It is, of course, also an error to fail to make a mark when a minor second is heard.

The first interval heard on each tape is the interval to be discriminated. If you forget the sound of it, you will be reminded every time you hear an interval followed by the high electronic tone. Soon you will become skillful in detecting the difference between this interval and the others on the tape. Think of the task as trying to make a tally mark just before each electronic sound, and only then.

These instructions sound complex, but the process will become clear as soon as the tape is begun.

Make the tally marks in a row until a mistake is made. Then start a new line below. The page will look something like this:

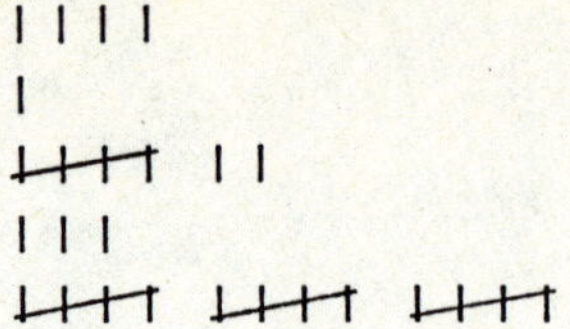

Try to make 15 correct marks in a row. As soon as you do this, go on to the next lesson, even if the tape is not finished. If necessary, rewind the tape to accomplish this goal.

SERIES A2

INTERVAL SIGHTSINGING

The purpose of this series is to develop the ability to sing from printed notation two tones that form various intervals. A printed score and tape recording are provided for each lesson. Intervals on the score are separated by barlines. When you start the tape recording, you will hear the first tone of an interval followed by two metronome clicks. With these two clicks, you should sing the first and second tones of the interval. Immediately after, you will hear on the tape the two pitches of the correct interval. Thus you will be able to judge whether or not you sang the interval correctly.

Depending on the range of your voice, you may find it necessary to sing in an octave different from that you hear on the tape. And you may find it necessary to change octaves in the course of the lesson. Sing in the most comfortable part of your vocal range at all times.

A2-1 Interval sightsinging: major and minor seconds

A2-2 Interval sightsinging: major and minor thirds

A2-3 Interval sightsinging: perfect and augmented fourths, perfect and diminished fifths

A2-4 Interval sightsinging: major and minor sixths

A2-5 Interval sightsinging: major and minor sevenths, perfect octaves

A2-6 Interval sightsinging: all intervals previously studied

A2-7 Interval sightsinging: all intervals previously studied

A2-8 Interval sightsinging: all intervals previously studied

A2-9 Interval sightsinging: all intervals previously studied

SERIES A3

MELODIC INTERVAL DICTATION

The purpose of this series is to develop the ability to write the second of two notes that form intervals you hear. A printed worksheet and tape recording are provided for each lesson.

For each interval, the first tone heard is given on the worksheet by a large note. Following this is a space in which you should write the second note after you hear the interval on the tape. To the right of this space, a small note indicates the correct answer.

To do a lesson, place a shield over the little note to the right. Listen to the tape, write the note that will complete the interval you heard, and only then slide the shield to the right to find the correct answer. You may stop the tape occasionally if you need more time. Be sure to make a committed response before looking at the right answer. Learning is much more effective when this is done.

Your response is correct if the note you have written is the same as the small note, or if it is enharmonic with it. Enharmonic tones are written differently, but refer to the same pitches. For example, F-sharp and G-flat sound the same, but are written differently.

A3-1 Melodic interval dictation: major and minor seconds
(COPY 1)

A3-1 Melodic interval dictation: major and minor seconds

(COPY 2)

A3-1 Melodic interval dictation: major and minor seconds

(COPY 3)

A3-2 Melodic interval dictation: major and minor thirds
(COPY 1)

A3-2 Melodic interval dictation: major and minor thirds
(COPY 2)

A3-2 Melodic interval dictation: major and minor thirds
(COPY 3)

A3-3 Melodic interval dictation: perfect and augmented fourths, perfect and diminished fifths

(COPY 1)

A3-3 Melodic interval dictation: perfect and augmented fourths, perfect and diminished fifths

(COPY 2)

A3-3 Melodic interval dictation: perfect and augmented fourths, perfect and diminished fifths
(COPY 3)

A3-4 Melodic interval dictation: major and minor sixths

(COPY 1)

A3-4 Melodic interval dictation: major and minor sixths
(COPY 2)

A3-4 Melodic interval dictation: major and minor sixths
(COPY 3)

A3-5 Melodic interval dictation: major and minor sevenths, perfect octaves

(COPY 1)

A3-5 Melodic interval dictation: major and minor sevenths, perfect octaves

(COPY 2)

A3-5 Melodic interval dictation: major and minor sevenths, perfect octaves
(COPY 3)

A3-6 Melodic interval dictation: all intervals previously studied

(COPY 1)

A3-6 Melodic interval dictation: all intervals previously studied

(COPY 2)

A3-6 Melodic interval dictation: all intervals previously studied

(COPY 3)

A3-7 Melodic interval dictation: all intervals previously studied

(COPY 1)

A3-7 Melodic interval dictation: all intervals previously studied

(COPY 2)

A3-7 Melodic interval dictation: all intervals previously studied

(COPY 3)

A3-8 Melodic interval dictation: all intervals previously studied

(COPY 1)

A3-8 Melodic interval dictation: all intervals previously studied

(COPY 2)

A3-8 Melodic interval dictation: all intervals previously studied

(COPY 3)

A3-9 Melodic interval dictation: all intervals previously studied

(COPY 1)

A3-9 Melodic interval dictation: all intervals previously studied

(COPY 2)

A3-9 Melodic interval dictation: all intervals previously studied
(COPY 3)

SERIES A4

MELODIC INTERVAL IDENTIFICATION

The purpose of this series is to develop the ability to identify melodic intervals formed by two tones that you hear. The following set of symbols will be used to identify the intervals.

m2	minor second	P5	perfect fifth
M2	major second	m6	minor sixth
m3	minor third	M6	major sixth
M3	major third	m7	minor seventh
P4	perfect fourth	M7	major seventh
T	tritone	P8	perfect octave

The letter *T* is used for the tritone because the tritone may be either a diminished fifth or an augmented fourth, and thus might be written in two ways.

A printed worksheet and a tape recording are provided for each lesson. On the worksheet, you should work across the page following each number in order. Use a shield to cover the correct answer until you have heard the interval on the tape and have written your answer. Move the shield to the right to find the correct answer, and then move on to the next interval to the right. You may stop the tape occasionally if you need more time.

A4-1 Melodic interval identification: major and minor seconds and thirds
(COPY 1)

1	____ m2	____ M2	____ m3	____ M3	____ M2	____ M3	____ m2	____ m3
2	____ M2	____ m2	____ m3	____ M2	____ M3	____ m2	____ m3	____ M3
3	____ m2	____ M2	____ m2	____ m3	____ M3	____ M2	____ m3	____ m2
4	____ m2	____ M2	____ M3	____ m3	____ M3	____ m3	____ M2	____ M3
5	____ m3	____ M3	____ m2	____ M2	____ m3	____ m2	____ M3	____ M2
6	____ M3	____ M2	____ m3	____ m2	____ M3	____ m3	____ M2	____ m2
7	____ m2	____ m2	____ M2	____ M2	____ m3	____ M3	____ M3	____ m3
8	____ M2	____ m2	____ M3	____ M2	____ m3	____ m3	____ m2	____ M3
9	____ m2	____ M2	____ M2	____ M3	____ m3	____ m3	____ M3	____ m2
10	____ m3	____ M3	____ M3	____ m3	____ m3	____ M3	____ M3	____ m3
11	____ M2	____ m2	____ m3	____ M3	____ m3	____ M3	____ m3	____ M2
12	____ m3	____ M3	____ m2	____ M2	____ m3	____ m2	____ M2	____ m2

A4-1 Melodic interval identification: major and minor seconds and thirds
(COPY 2)

1	____ m2	____ M2	____ m3	____ M3	____ M2	____ M3	____ m2	____ m3
2	____ M2	____ m2	____ m3	____ M2	____ M3	____ m2	____ m3	____ M3
3	____ m2	____ M2	____ m2	____ m3	____ M3	____ M2	____ m3	____ m2
4	____ m2	____ M2	____ M3	____ m3	____ M3	____ m3	____ M2	____ M3
5	____ m3	____ M3	____ m2	____ M2	____ m3	____ m2	____ M3	____ M2
6	____ M3	____ M2	____ m3	____ m2	____ M3	____ m3	____ M2	____ m2
7	____ m2	____ m2	____ M2	____ M2	____ m3	____ M3	____ M3	____ m3
8	____ M2	____ m2	____ M3	____ M2	____ m3	____ m3	____ m2	____ M3
9	____ m2	____ M2	____ M2	____ M3	____ m3	____ m3	____ M3	____ m2
10	____ m3	____ M3	____ M3	____ m3	____ m3	____ M3	____ M3	____ m3
11	____ M2	____ m2	____ m3	____ M3	____ m3	____ M3	____ m3	____ M2
12	____ m3	____ M3	____ m2	____ M2	____ m3	____ m2	____ M2	____ m2

A4-I Melodic interval identification: major and minor seconds and thirds
(COPY 3)

1	____ m2	____ M2	____ m3	____ M3	____ M2	____ M3	____ m2	____ m3
2	____ M2	____ m2	____ m3	____ M2	____ M3	____ m2	____ m3	____ M3
3	____ m2	____ M2	____ m2	____ m3	____ M3	____ M2	____ m3	____ m2
4	____ m2	____ M2	____ M3	____ m3	____ M3	____ m3	____ M2	____ M3
5	____ m3	____ M3	____ m2	____ M2	____ m3	____ m2	____ M3	____ M2
6	____ M3	____ M2	____ m3	____ m2	____ M3	____ m3	____ M2	____ m2
7	____ m2	____ m2	____ M2	____ M2	____ m3	____ M3	____ M3	____ m3
8	____ M2	____ m2	____ M3	____ M2	____ m3	____ m3	____ m2	____ M3
9	____ m2	____ M2	____ M2	____ M3	____ m3	____ m3	____ M3	____ m2
10	____ m3	____ M3	____ M3	____ m3	____ m3	____ M3	____ M3	____ m3
11	____ M2	____ m2	____ m3	____ M3	____ m3	____ M3	____ m3	____ M2
12	____ m3	____ M3	____ m2	____ M2	____ m3	____ m2	____ M2	____ m2

A4-I Melodic interval identification: major and minor seconds and thirds
(COPY 4)

1	____ m2	____ M2	____ m3	____ M3	____ M2	____ M3	____ m2	____ m3
2	____ M2	____ m2	____ m3	____ M2	____ M3	____ m2	____ m3	____ M3
3	____ m2	____ M2	____ m2	____ m3	____ M3	____ M2	____ m3	____ m2
4	____ m2	____ M2	____ M3	____ m3	____ M3	____ m3	____ M2	____ M3
5	____ m3	____ M3	____ m2	____ M2	____ m3	____ m2	____ M3	____ M2
6	____ M3	____ M2	____ m3	____ m2	____ M3	____ m3	____ M2	____ m2
7	____ m2	____ m2	____ M2	____ M2	____ m3	____ M3	____ M3	____ m3
8	____ M2	____ m2	____ M3	____ M2	____ m3	____ m3	____ m2	____ M3
9	____ m2	____ M2	____ M2	____ M3	____ m3	____ m3	____ M3	____ m2
10	____ m3	____ M3	____ M3	____ m3	____ m3	____ M3	____ M3	____ m3
11	____ M2	____ m2	____ m3	____ M3	____ m3	____ M3	____ m3	____ M2
12	____ m3	____ M3	____ m2	____ M2	____ m3	____ m2	____ M2	____ m2

A4-2 Melodic interval identification: major thirds, perfect fourths and fifths, tritones

(COPY 1)

1 ____ P4 ____ P5 ____ T ____ P4 ____ M3 ____ P4 ____ P5 ____ P4

2 ____ P4 ____ P4 ____ P4 ____ P5 ____ P4 ____ P5 ____ P4 ____ P5

3 ____ P4 ____ P5 ____ M3 ____ P4 ____ T ____ P5 ____ P4 ____ P5

4 ____ P4 ____ P4 ____ P4 ____ P5 ____ P4 ____ P5 ____ P4 ____ P5

5 ____ P5 ____ P4 ____ P5 ____ P4 ____ P4 ____ P5 ____ P5 ____ P4

6 ____ P5 ____ P4 ____ P4 ____ P5 ____ P5 ____ P4 ____ P5 ____ P5

7 ____ P5 ____ M3 ____ P4 ____ T ____ P5 ____ P5 ____ T ____ P4

8 ____ M3 ____ P4 ____ P5 ____ T ____ P5 ____ P4 ____ M3 ____ P4

9 ____ P4 ____ P4 ____ P5 ____ P4 ____ T ____ P5 ____ P4 ____ T

10 ____ P5 ____ P4 ____ T ____ P5 ____ P5 ____ P4 ____ T ____ P5

11 ____ P5 ____ P4 ____ M3 ____ P4 ____ T ____ P4 ____ T ____ P4

12 ____ P5 ____ P5 ____ T ____ P4 ____ P5 ____ P5 ____ T ____ P5

A4-2 Melodic interval identification: major thirds, perfect fourths and fifths, tritones

(COPY 2)

1 ____ P4 ____ P5 ____ T ____ P4 ____ M3 ____ P4 ____ P5 ____ P4

2 ____ P4 ____ P4 ____ P4 ____ P5 ____ P4 ____ P5 ____ P4 ____ P5

3 ____ P4 ____ P5 ____ M3 ____ P4 ____ T ____ P5 ____ P4 ____ P5

4 ____ P4 ____ P4 ____ P4 ____ P5 ____ P4 ____ P5 ____ P4 ____ P5

5 ____ P5 ____ P4 ____ P5 ____ P4 ____ P4 ____ P5 ____ P5 ____ P4

6 ____ P5 ____ P4 ____ P4 ____ P5 ____ P5 ____ P4 ____ P5 ____ P5

7 ____ P5 ____ M3 ____ P4 ____ T ____ P5 ____ P5 ____ T ____ P4

8 ____ M3 ____ P4 ____ P5 ____ T ____ P5 ____ P4 ____ M3 ____ P4

9 ____ P4 ____ P4 ____ P5 ____ P4 ____ T ____ P5 ____ P4 ____ T

10 ____ P5 ____ P4 ____ T ____ P5 ____ P5 ____ P4 ____ T ____ P5

11 ____ P5 ____ P4 ____ M3 ____ P4 ____ T ____ P4 ____ T ____ P4

12 ____ P5 ____ P5 ____ T ____ P4 ____ P5 ____ P5 ____ T ____ P5

A4-2 (COPY 3) Melodic interval identification: major thirds, perfect fourths and fifths, tritones

1	___ P4	___ P5	___ T	___ P4	___ M3	___ P4	___ P5	___ P4
2	___ P4	___ P4	___ P4	___ P5	___ P4	___ P5	___ P4	___ P5
3	___ P4	___ P5	___ M3	___ P4	___ T	___ P5	___ P4	___ P5
4	___ P4	___ P4	___ P4	___ P5	___ P4	___ P5	___ P4	___ P5
5	___ P5	___ P4	___ P5	___ P4	___ P4	___ P5	___ P5	___ P4
6	___ P5	___ P4	___ P4	___ P5	___ P5	___ P4	___ P5	___ P5
7	___ P5	___ M3	___ P4	___ T	___ P5	___ P5	___ T	___ P4
8	___ M3	___ P4	___ P5	___ T	___ P5	___ P4	___ M3	___ P4
9	___ P4	___ P4	___ P5	___ P4	___ T	___ P5	___ P4	___ T
10	___ P5	___ P4	___ T	___ P5	___ P5	___ P4	___ T	___ P5
11	___ P5	___ P4	___ M3	___ P4	___ T	___ P4	___ T	___ P4
12	___ P5	___ P5	___ T	___ P4	___ P5	___ P5	___ T	___ P5

A4-2 (COPY 4) Melodic interval identification: major thirds, perfect fourths and fifths, tritones

1	___ P4	___ P5	___ T	___ P4	___ M3	___ P4	___ P5	___ P4
2	___ P4	___ P4	___ P4	___ P5	___ P4	___ P5	___ P4	___ P5
3	___ P4	___ P5	___ M3	___ P4	___ T	___ P5	___ P4	___ P5
4	___ P4	___ P4	___ P4	___ P5	___ P4	___ P5	___ P4	___ P5
5	___ P5	___ P4	___ P5	___ P4	___ P4	___ P5	___ P5	___ P4
6	___ P5	___ P4	___ P4	___ P5	___ P5	___ P4	___ P5	___ P5
7	___ P5	___ M3	___ P4	___ T	___ P5	___ P5	___ T	___ P4
8	___ M3	___ P4	___ P5	___ T	___ P5	___ P4	___ M3	___ P4
9	___ P4	___ P4	___ P5	___ P4	___ T	___ P5	___ P4	___ T
10	___ P5	___ P4	___ T	___ P5	___ P5	___ P4	___ T	___ P5
11	___ P5	___ P4	___ M3	___ P4	___ T	___ P4	___ T	___ P4
12	___ P5	___ P5	___ T	___ P4	___ P5	___ P5	___ T	___ P5

A4-3 Melodic interval identification: perfect fifths, major and minor sixths

(COPY 1)

1 ____ M6 ____ m6 ____ P5 ____ M6 ____ m6 ____ M6 ____ P5 ____ m6

2 ____ M6 ____ P5 ____ m6 ____ M6 ____ M6 ____ P5 ____ m6 ____ M6

3 ____ m6 ____ P5 ____ M6 ____ m6 ____ P5 ____ M6 ____ P5 ____ m6

4 ____ m6 ____ M6 ____ M6 ____ m6 ____ M6 ____ m6 ____ M6 ____ m6

5 ____ M6 ____ m6 ____ M6 ____ M6 ____ M6 ____ m6 ____ m6 ____ M6

6 ____ M6 ____ P5 ____ m6 ____ M6 ____ M6 ____ P5 ____ m6 ____ m6

7 ____ M6 ____ m6 ____ P5 ____ M6 ____ P5 ____ M6 ____ P5 ____ m6

8 ____ P5 ____ m6 ____ P5 ____ M6 ____ M6 ____ m6 ____ P5 ____ m6

9 ____ M6 ____ P5 ____ m6 ____ P5 ____ m6 ____ P5 ____ M6 ____ M6

10 ____ M6 ____ m6 ____ M6 ____ P5 ____ m6 ____ M6 ____ M6 ____ m6

11 ____ M6 ____ m6 ____ P5 ____ P5 ____ M6 ____ m6 ____ M6 ____ P5

12 ____ P5 ____ M6 ____ m6 ____ P5 ____ M6 ____ m6 ____ M6 ____ P5

A4-3 Melodic interval identification: perfect fifths, major and minor sixths

(COPY 2)

1 ____ M6 ____ m6 ____ P5 ____ M6 ____ m6 ____ M6 ____ P5 ____ m6

2 ____ M6 ____ P5 ____ m6 ____ M6 ____ M6 ____ P5 ____ m6 ____ M6

3 ____ m6 ____ P5 ____ M6 ____ m6 ____ P5 ____ M6 ____ P5 ____ m6

4 ____ m6 ____ M6 ____ M6 ____ m6 ____ M6 ____ m6 ____ M6 ____ m6

5 ____ M6 ____ m6 ____ M6 ____ M6 ____ M6 ____ m6 ____ m6 ____ M6

6 ____ M6 ____ P5 ____ m6 ____ M6 ____ M6 ____ P5 ____ m6 ____ m6

7 ____ M6 ____ m6 ____ P5 ____ M6 ____ P5 ____ M6 ____ P5 ____ m6

8 ____ P5 ____ m6 ____ P5 ____ M6 ____ M6 ____ m6 ____ P5 ____ m6

9 ____ M6 ____ P5 ____ m6 ____ P5 ____ m6 ____ P5 ____ M6 ____ M6

10 ____ M6 ____ m6 ____ M6 ____ P5 ____ m6 ____ M6 ____ M6 ____ m6

11 ____ M6 ____ m6 ____ P5 ____ P5 ____ M6 ____ m6 ____ M6 ____ P5

12 ____ P5 ____ M6 ____ m6 ____ P5 ____ M6 ____ m6 ____ M6 ____ P5

A4-3 Melodic interval identification: perfect fifths, major and minor sixths
(COPY 3)

1	____ M6	____ m6	____ P5	____ M6	____ m6	____ M6	____ P5	____ m6
2	____ M6	____ P5	____ m6	____ M6	____ M6	____ P5	____ m6	____ M6
3	____ m6	____ P5	____ M6	____ m6	____ P5	____ M6	____ P5	____ m6
4	____ m6	____ M6	____ M6	____ m6	____ M6	____ m6	____ M6	____ m6
5	____ M6	____ m6	____ M6	____ M6	____ M6	____ m6	____ m6	____ M6
6	____ M6	____ P5	____ m6	____ M6	____ M6	____ P5	____ m6	____ m6
7	____ M6	____ m6	____ P5	____ M6	____ P5	____ M6	____ P5	____ m6
8	____ P5	____ m6	____ P5	____ M6	____ M6	____ m6	____ P5	____ m6
9	____ M6	____ P5	____ m6	____ P5	____ m6	____ P5	____ M6	____ M6
10	____ M6	____ m6	____ M6	____ P5	____ m6	____ M6	____ M6	____ m6
11	____ M6	____ m6	____ P5	____ P5	____ M6	____ m6	____ M6	____ P5
12	____ P5	____ M6	____ m6	____ P5	____ M6	____ m6	____ M6	____ P5

A4-3 Melodic interval identification: perfect fifths, major and minor sixths
(COPY 4)

1	____ M6	____ m6	____ P5	____ M6	____ m6	____ M6	____ P5	____ m6
2	____ M6	____ P5	____ m6	____ M6	____ M6	____ P5	____ m6	____ M6
3	____ m6	____ P5	____ M6	____ m6	____ P5	____ M6	____ P5	____ m6
4	____ m6	____ M6	____ M6	____ m6	____ M6	____ m6	____ M6	____ m6
5	____ M6	____ m6	____ M6	____ M6	____ M6	____ m6	____ m6	____ M6
6	____ M6	____ P5	____ m6	____ M6	____ M6	____ P5	____ m6	____ m6
7	____ M6	____ m6	____ P5	____ M6	____ P5	____ M6	____ P5	____ m6
8	____ P5	____ m6	____ P5	____ M6	____ M6	____ m6	____ P5	____ m6
9	____ M6	____ P5	____ m6	____ P5	____ m6	____ P5	____ M6	____ M6
10	____ M6	____ m6	____ M6	____ P5	____ m6	____ M6	____ M6	____ m6
11	____ M6	____ m6	____ P5	____ P5	____ M6	____ m6	____ M6	____ P5
12	____ P5	____ M6	____ m6	____ P5	____ M6	____ m6	____ M6	____ P5

A4-4 Melodic interval identification: major sixths, major and minor sevenths, perfect octaves

(COPY 1)

1	___ P8	___ M7	___ m7	___ M6	___ P8	___ m7	___ M7	___ P8
2	___ P8	___ M7	___ m7	___ P8	___ M7	___ P8	___ m7	___ M7
3	___ M7	___ m7	___ P8	___ M7	___ m7	___ m7	___ M7	___ M6
4	___ m7	___ M7	___ M7	___ m7	___ P8	___ m7	___ M7	___ M7
5	___ m7	___ M7	___ P8	___ m7	___ M7	___ M7	___ m7	___ M6
6	___ P8	___ m7	___ P8	___ M7	___ P8	___ m7	___ P8	___ M7
7	___ m7	___ P8	___ M7	___ M6	___ M7	___ m7	___ P8	___ M7
8	___ P8	___ m7	___ P8	___ m7	___ M6	___ M6	___ m7	___ M7
9	___ m7	___ M7	___ m7	___ M6	___ M7	___ m7	___ M7	___ P8
10	___ M6	___ m7	___ P8	___ M7	___ M7	___ M7	___ m7	___ P8
11	___ P8	___ m7	___ M6	___ m7	___ P8	___ M6	___ m7	___ M7
12	___ P8	___ m7	___ P8	___ M7	___ M7	___ m7	___ M6	___ P8

A4-4 Melodic interval identification: major sixths, major and minor sevenths, perfect octaves

(COPY 2)

1	___ P8	___ M7	___ m7	___ M6	___ P8	___ m7	___ M7	___ P8
2	___ P8	___ M7	___ m7	___ P8	___ M7	___ P8	___ m7	___ M7
3	___ M7	___ m7	___ P8	___ M7	___ m7	___ m7	___ M7	___ M6
4	___ m7	___ M7	___ M7	___ m7	___ P8	___ m7	___ M7	___ M7
5	___ m7	___ M7	___ P8	___ m7	___ M7	___ M7	___ m7	___ M6
6	___ P8	___ m7	___ P8	___ M7	___ P8	___ m7	___ P8	___ M7
7	___ m7	___ P8	___ M7	___ M6	___ M7	___ m7	___ P8	___ M7
8	___ P8	___ m7	___ P8	___ m7	___ M6	___ M6	___ m7	___ M7
9	___ m7	___ M7	___ m7	___ M6	___ M7	___ m7	___ M7	___ P8
10	___ M6	___ m7	___ P8	___ M7	___ M7	___ M7	___ m7	___ P8
11	___ P8	___ m7	___ M6	___ m7	___ P8	___ M6	___ m7	___ M7
12	___ P8	___ m7	___ P8	___ M7	___ M7	___ m7	___ M6	___ P8

A4-4 (COPY 3) Melodic interval identification: major sixths, major and minor sevenths, perfect octaves

1 ____ P8 ____ M7 ____ m7 ____ M6 ____ P8 ____ m7 ____ M7 ____ P8
2 ____ P8 ____ M7 ____ m7 ____ P8 ____ M7 ____ P8 ____ m7 ____ M7
3 ____ M7 ____ m7 ____ P8 ____ M7 ____ m7 ____ m7 ____ M7 ____ M6
4 ____ m7 ____ M7 ____ M7 ____ m7 ____ P8 ____ m7 ____ M7 ____ M7
5 ____ m7 ____ M7 ____ P8 ____ m7 ____ M7 ____ M7 ____ m7 ____ M6
6 ____ P8 ____ m7 ____ P8 ____ M7 ____ P8 ____ m7 ____ P8 ____ M7
7 ____ m7 ____ P8 ____ M7 ____ M6 ____ M7 ____ m7 ____ P8 ____ M7
8 ____ P8 ____ m7 ____ P8 ____ m7 ____ M6 ____ M6 ____ m7 ____ M7
9 ____ m7 ____ M7 ____ m7 ____ M6 ____ M7 ____ m7 ____ M7 ____ P8
10 ____ M6 ____ m7 ____ P8 ____ M7 ____ M7 ____ M7 ____ m7 ____ P8
11 ____ P8 ____ m7 ____ M6 ____ m7 ____ P8 ____ M6 ____ m7 ____ M7
12 ____ P8 ____ m7 ____ P8 ____ M7 ____ M7 ____ m7 ____ M6 ____ P8

A4-4 (COPY 4) Melodic interval identification: major sixths, major and minor sevenths, perfect octaves

1 ____ P8 ____ M7 ____ m7 ____ M6 ____ P8 ____ m7 ____ M7 ____ P8
2 ____ P8 ____ M7 ____ m7 ____ P8 ____ M7 ____ P8 ____ m7 ____ M7
3 ____ M7 ____ m7 ____ P8 ____ M7 ____ m7 ____ m7 ____ M7 ____ M6
4 ____ m7 ____ M7 ____ M7 ____ m7 ____ P8 ____ m7 ____ M7 ____ M7
5 ____ m7 ____ M7 ____ P8 ____ m7 ____ M7 ____ M7 ____ m7 ____ M6
6 ____ P8 ____ m7 ____ P8 ____ M7 ____ P8 ____ m7 ____ P8 ____ M7
7 ____ m7 ____ P8 ____ M7 ____ M6 ____ M7 ____ m7 ____ P8 ____ M7
8 ____ P8 ____ m7 ____ P8 ____ m7 ____ M6 ____ M6 ____ m7 ____ M7
9 ____ m7 ____ M7 ____ m7 ____ M6 ____ M7 ____ m7 ____ M7 ____ P8
10 ____ M6 ____ m7 ____ P8 ____ M7 ____ M7 ____ M7 ____ m7 ____ P8
11 ____ P8 ____ m7 ____ M6 ____ m7 ____ P8 ____ M6 ____ m7 ____ M7
12 ____ P8 ____ m7 ____ P8 ____ M7 ____ M7 ____ m7 ____ M6 ____ P8

A4-5 Melodic interval identification: all intervals previously studied

(COPY 1)

1	____ P8	____ P5	____ M3	____ P4	____ M2	____ P5	____ P4	____ P8
2	____ P5	____ M3	____ M2	____ T	____ P5	____ M6	____ M7	____ P8
3	____ P8	____ P5	____ M3	____ P4	____ M6	____ P5	____ M7	____ M2
4	____ P8	____ M3	____ P4	____ P5	____ T	____ P4	____ M7	____ P8
5	____ M2	____ m2	____ M3	____ m3	____ P5	____ M6	____ m6	____ P4
6	____ M7	____ m7	____ M6	____ m6	____ M3	____ m3	____ M6	____ m6
7	____ m7	____ M7	____ M6	____ P4	____ m6	____ M3	____ P5	____ m3
8	____ m2	____ P5	____ m7	____ m3	____ m6	____ m7	____ P4	____ T
9	____ P5	____ T	____ P4	____ M2	____ M6	____ m3	____ M7	____ P4
10	____ m7	____ M3	____ M6	____ m3	____ P4	____ M7	____ P5	____ P8
11	____ M6	____ P5	____ M6	____ P4	____ T	____ P5	____ M3	____ P4
12	____ M3	____ m6	____ P4	____ M3	____ P5	____ m2	____ M7	____ P5

A4-5 Melodic interval identification: all intervals previously studied

(COPY 2)

1	____ P8	____ P5	____ M3	____ P4	____ M2	____ P5	____ P4	____ P8
2	____ P5	____ M3	____ M2	____ T	____ P5	____ M6	____ M7	____ P8
3	____ P8	____ P5	____ M3	____ P4	____ M6	____ P5	____ M7	____ M2
4	____ P8	____ M3	____ P4	____ P5	____ T	____ P4	____ M7	____ P8
5	____ M2	____ m2	____ M3	____ m3	____ P5	____ M6	____ m6	____ P4
6	____ M7	____ m7	____ M6	____ m6	____ M3	____ m3	____ M6	____ m6
7	____ m7	____ M7	____ M6	____ P4	____ m6	____ M3	____ P5	____ m3
8	____ m2	____ P5	____ m7	____ m3	____ m6	____ m7	____ P4	____ T
9	____ P5	____ T	____ P4	____ M2	____ M6	____ m3	____ M7	____ P4
10	____ m7	____ M3	____ M6	____ m3	____ P4	____ M7	____ P5	____ P8
11	____ M6	____ P5	____ M6	____ P4	____ T	____ P5	____ M3	____ P4
12	____ M3	____ m6	____ P4	____ M3	____ P5	____ m2	____ M7	____ P5

A4-5 Melodic interval identification: all intervals previously studied

(COPY 3)

1	____ P8	____ P5	____ M3	____ P4	____ M2	____ P5	____ P4	____ P8
2	____ P5	____ M3	____ M2	____ T	____ P5	____ M6	____ M7	____ P8
3	____ P8	____ P5	____ M3	____ P4	____ M6	____ P5	____ M7	____ M2
4	____ P8	____ M3	____ P4	____ P5	____ T	____ P4	____ M7	____ P8
5	____ M2	____ m2	____ M3	____ m3	____ P5	____ M6	____ m6	____ P4
6	____ M7	____ m7	____ M6	____ m6	____ M3	____ m3	____ M6	____ m6
7	____ m7	____ M7	____ M6	____ P4	____ m6	____ M3	____ P5	____ m3
8	____ m2	____ P5	____ m7	____ m3	____ m6	____ m7	____ P4	____ T
9	____ P5	____ T	____ P4	____ M2	____ M6	____ m3	____ M7	____ P4
10	____ m7	____ M3	____ M6	____ m3	____ P4	____ M7	____ P5	____ P8
11	____ M6	____ P5	____ M6	____ P4	____ T	____ P5	____ M3	____ P4
12	____ M3	____ m6	____ P4	____ M3	____ P5	____ m2	____ M7	____ P5

A4-5 Melodic interval identification: all intervals previously studied

(COPY 4)

1	____ P8	____ P5	____ M3	____ P4	____ M2	____ P5	____ P4	____ P8
2	____ P5	____ M3	____ M2	____ T	____ P5	____ M6	____ M7	____ P8
3	____ P8	____ P5	____ M3	____ P4	____ M6	____ P5	____ M7	____ M2
4	____ P8	____ M3	____ P4	____ P5	____ T	____ P4	____ M7	____ P8
5	____ M2	____ m2	____ M3	____ m3	____ P5	____ M6	____ m6	____ P4
6	____ M7	____ m7	____ M6	____ m6	____ M3	____ m3	____ M6	____ m6
7	____ m7	____ M7	____ M6	____ P4	____ m6	____ M3	____ P5	____ m3
8	____ m2	____ P5	____ m7	____ m3	____ m6	____ m7	____ P4	____ T
9	____ P5	____ T	____ P4	____ M2	____ M6	____ m3	____ M7	____ P4
10	____ m7	____ M3	____ M6	____ m3	____ P4	____ M7	____ P5	____ P8
11	____ M6	____ P5	____ M6	____ P4	____ T	____ P5	____ M3	____ P4
12	____ M3	____ m6	____ P4	____ M3	____ P5	____ m2	____ M7	____ P5

A4-6 Melodic interval identification: all intervals previously studied
(COPY 1)

1	____ P8	____ P5	____ P4	____ m3	____ M3	____ M6	____ M2	____ M7
2	____ M2	____ P8	____ P5	____ M3	____ P4	____ M6	____ M7	____ P8
3	____ P8	____ P5	____ T	____ P4	____ m2	____ P5	____ M6	____ m6
4	____ m2	____ M2	____ M3	____ P5	____ P8	____ M7	____ P4	____ M6
5	____ P8	____ P4	____ M3	____ P5	____ T	____ M3	____ P5	____ P4
6	____ P5	____ P4	____ M3	____ P5	____ T	____ M7	____ P8	____ P5
7	____ P4	____ M3	____ M3	____ P5	____ P4	____ m2	____ P5	____ m6
8	____ P5	____ M6	____ M7	____ M7	____ m6	____ P5	____ m6	____ M3
9	____ m3	____ m7	____ P5	____ M7	____ P5	____ M6	____ m6	____ P5
10	____ M3	____ M7	____ M6	____ M3	____ m3	____ m6	____ M6	____ P5
11	____ M6	____ P5	____ T	____ m6	____ M2	____ P4	____ m6	____ m6
12	____ M2	____ M3	____ T	____ P4	____ P4	____ m7	____ P4	____ m6

A4-6 Melodic interval identification: all intervals previously studied
(COPY 2)

1	____ P8	____ P5	____ P4	____ m3	____ M3	____ M6	____ M2	____ M7
2	____ M2	____ P8	____ P5	____ M3	____ P4	____ M6	____ M7	____ P8
3	____ P8	____ P5	____ T	____ P4	____ m2	____ P5	____ M6	____ m6
4	____ m2	____ M2	____ M3	____ P5	____ P8	____ M7	____ P4	____ M6
5	____ P8	____ P4	____ M3	____ P5	____ T	____ M3	____ P5	____ P4
6	____ P5	____ P4	____ M3	____ P5	____ T	____ M7	____ P8	____ P5
7	____ P4	____ M3	____ M3	____ P5	____ P4	____ m2	____ P5	____ m6
8	____ P5	____ M6	____ M7	____ M7	____ m6	____ P5	____ m6	____ M3
9	____ m3	____ m7	____ P5	____ M7	____ P5	____ M6	____ m6	____ P5
10	____ M3	____ M7	____ M6	____ M3	____ m3	____ m6	____ M6	____ P5
11	____ M6	____ P5	____ T	____ m6	____ M2	____ P4	____ m6	____ m6
12	____ M2	____ M3	____ T	____ P4	____ P4	____ m7	____ P4	____ m6

A4-6 Melodic interval identification: all intervals previously studied

(COPY 3)

1 ____ P8 ____ P5 ____ P4 ____ m3 ____ M3 ____ M6 ____ M2 ____ M7

2 ____ M2 ____ P8 ____ P5 ____ M3 ____ P4 ____ M6 ____ M7 ____ P8

3 ____ P8 ____ P5 ____ T ____ P4 ____ m2 ____ P5 ____ M6 ____ m6

4 ____ m2 ____ M2 ____ M3 ____ P5 ____ P8 ____ M7 ____ P4 ____ M6

5 ____ P8 ____ P4 ____ M3 ____ P5 ____ T ____ M3 ____ P5 ____ P4

6 ____ P5 ____ P4 ____ M3 ____ P5 ____ T ____ M7 ____ P8 ____ P5

7 ____ P4 ____ M3 ____ M3 ____ P5 ____ P4 ____ m2 ____ P5 ____ m6

8 ____ P5 ____ M6 ____ M7 ____ M7 ____ m6 ____ P5 ____ m6 ____ M3

9 ____ m3 ____ m7 ____ P5 ____ M7 ____ P5 ____ M6 ____ m6 ____ P5

10 ____ M3 ____ M7 ____ M6 ____ M3 ____ m3 ____ m6 ____ M6 ____ P5

11 ____ M6 ____ P5 ____ T ____ m6 ____ M2 ____ P4 ____ m6 ____ m6

12 ____ M2 ____ M3 ____ T ____ P4 ____ P4 ____ m7 ____ P4 ____ m6

A4-6 Melodic interval identification: all intervals previously studied

(COPY 4)

1 ____ P8 ____ P5 ____ P4 ____ m3 ____ M3 ____ M6 ____ M2 ____ M7

2 ____ M2 ____ P8 ____ P5 ____ M3 ____ P4 ____ M6 ____ M7 ____ P8

3 ____ P8 ____ P5 ____ T ____ P4 ____ m2 ____ P5 ____ M6 ____ m6

4 ____ m2 ____ M2 ____ M3 ____ P5 ____ P8 ____ M7 ____ P4 ____ M6

5 ____ P8 ____ P4 ____ M3 ____ P5 ____ T ____ M3 ____ P5 ____ P4

6 ____ P5 ____ P4 ____ M3 ____ P5 ____ T ____ M7 ____ P8 ____ P5

7 ____ P4 ____ M3 ____ M3 ____ P5 ____ P4 ____ m2 ____ P5 ____ m6

8 ____ P5 ____ M6 ____ M7 ____ M7 ____ m6 ____ P5 ____ m6 ____ M3

9 ____ m3 ____ m7 ____ P5 ____ M7 ____ P5 ____ M6 ____ m6 ____ P5

10 ____ M3 ____ M7 ____ M6 ____ M3 ____ m3 ____ m6 ____ M6 ____ P5

11 ____ M6 ____ P5 ____ T ____ m6 ____ M2 ____ P4 ____ m6 ____ m6

12 ____ M2 ____ M3 ____ T ____ P4 ____ P4 ____ m7 ____ P4 ____ m6

A4-7 Melodic interval identification: all intervals previously studied

(COPY 1)

1	___ P5	___ M3	___ m3	___ P4	___ P5	___ M2	___ m2	___ P5
2	___ M6	___ m3	___ P5	___ m6	___ P5	___ M3	___ m3	___ P4
3	___ P4	___ P5	___ M6	___ M2	___ P8	___ P5	___ m6	___ M7
4	___ P8	___ M2	___ M7	___ M3	___ P4	___ T	___ P5	___ P4
5	___ M7	___ M3	___ m7	___ P5	___ m6	___ M7	___ M3	___ m3
6	___ P5	___ M6	___ P5	___ m6	___ M3	___ m2	___ P5	___ m6
7	___ P8	___ m7	___ P5	___ M6	___ m3	___ M3	___ P5	___ m6
8	___ P4	___ T	___ M7	___ P5	___ M6	___ m7	___ P5	___ T
9	___ M3	___ m3	___ M2	___ P5	___ m6	___ M7	___ M6	___ P4
10	___ P5	___ m6	___ P4	___ T	___ P4	___ P5	___ M6	___ P5
11	___ M2	___ m7	___ m6	___ M6	___ P4	___ T	___ m3	___ m3
12	___ T	___ M6	___ m6	___ m3	___ M7	___ m7	___ m3	___ m6

A4-7 Melodic interval identification: all intervals previously studied

(COPY 2)

1	___ P5	___ M3	___ m3	___ P4	___ P5	___ M2	___ m2	___ P5
2	___ M6	___ m3	___ P5	___ m6	___ P5	___ M3	___ m3	___ P4
3	___ P4	___ P5	___ M6	___ M2	___ P8	___ P5	___ m6	___ M7
4	___ P8	___ M2	___ M7	___ M3	___ P4	___ T	___ P5	___ P4
5	___ M7	___ M3	___ m7	___ P5	___ m6	___ M7	___ M3	___ m3
6	___ P5	___ M6	___ P5	___ m6	___ M3	___ m2	___ P5	___ m6
7	___ P8	___ m7	___ P5	___ M6	___ m3	___ M3	___ P5	___ m6
8	___ P4	___ T	___ M7	___ P5	___ M6	___ m7	___ P5	___ T
9	___ M3	___ m3	___ M2	___ P5	___ m6	___ M7	___ M6	___ P4
10	___ P5	___ m6	___ P4	___ T	___ P4	___ P5	___ M6	___ P5
11	___ M2	___ m7	___ m6	___ M6	___ P4	___ T	___ m3	___ m3
12	___ T	___ M6	___ m6	___ m3	___ M7	___ m7	___ m3	___ m6

A4-7 Melodic interval identification: all intervals previously studied
(COPY 3)

1 ____ P5 ____ M3 ____ m3 ____ P4 ____ P5 ____ M2 ____ m2 ____ P5
2 ____ M6 ____ m3 ____ P5 ____ m6 ____ P5 ____ M3 ____ m3 ____ P4
3 ____ P4 ____ P5 ____ M6 ____ M2 ____ P8 ____ P5 ____ m6 ____ M7
4 ____ P8 ____ M2 ____ M7 ____ M3 ____ P4 ____ T ____ P5 ____ P4
5 ____ M7 ____ M3 ____ m7 ____ P5 ____ m6 ____ M7 ____ M3 ____ m3
6 ____ P5 ____ M6 ____ P5 ____ m6 ____ M3 ____ m2 ____ P5 ____ m6
7 ____ P8 ____ m7 ____ P5 ____ M6 ____ m3 ____ M3 ____ P5 ____ m6
8 ____ P4 ____ T ____ M7 ____ P5 ____ M6 ____ m7 ____ P5 ____ T
9 ____ M3 ____ m3 ____ M2 ____ P5 ____ m6 ____ M7 ____ M6 ____ P4
10 ____ P5 ____ m6 ____ P4 ____ T ____ P4 ____ P5 ____ M6 ____ P5
11 ____ M2 ____ m7 ____ m6 ____ M6 ____ P4 ____ T ____ m3 ____ m3
12 ____ T ____ M6 ____ m6 ____ m3 ____ M7 ____ m7 ____ m3 ____ m6

A4-7 Melodic interval identification: all intervals previously studied
(COPY 4)

1 ____ P5 ____ M3 ____ m3 ____ P4 ____ P5 ____ M2 ____ m2 ____ P5
2 ____ M6 ____ m3 ____ P5 ____ m6 ____ P5 ____ M3 ____ m3 ____ P4
3 ____ P4 ____ P5 ____ M6 ____ M2 ____ P8 ____ P5 ____ m6 ____ M7
4 ____ P8 ____ M2 ____ M7 ____ M3 ____ P4 ____ T ____ P5 ____ P4
5 ____ M7 ____ M3 ____ m7 ____ P5 ____ m6 ____ M7 ____ M3 ____ m3
6 ____ P5 ____ M6 ____ P5 ____ m6 ____ M3 ____ m2 ____ P5 ____ m6
7 ____ P8 ____ m7 ____ P5 ____ M6 ____ m3 ____ M3 ____ P5 ____ m6
8 ____ P4 ____ T ____ M7 ____ P5 ____ M6 ____ m7 ____ P5 ____ T
9 ____ M3 ____ m3 ____ M2 ____ P5 ____ m6 ____ M7 ____ M6 ____ P4
10 ____ P5 ____ m6 ____ P4 ____ T ____ P4 ____ P5 ____ M6 ____ P5
11 ____ M2 ____ m7 ____ m6 ____ M6 ____ P4 ____ T ____ m3 ____ m3
12 ____ T ____ M6 ____ m6 ____ m3 ____ M7 ____ m7 ____ m3 ____ m6

SERIES A5

HARMONIC INTERVAL DISCRIMINATION

The purpose of this series is to develop the ability to discriminate between harmonic intervals when they are heard.

The procedure is the same as for Series A1. Each lesson in this series is devoted to a particular interval. There is a tape recording for each lesson, but no worksheet. Scrap paper can be used for answers.

On the tape you will hear a variety of intervals. The task is to recognize the particular interval to which the lesson is devoted, and to respond by making a mark on the paper. You do not need to indicate the name of the interval, only to recognize the sound of it. For example, the first lesson is devoted to the interval of the minor second—that is, two tones a half-step apart. This interval is mixed in with other intervals. Sometimes the intervals will be high, sometimes low or in the middle register. But whenever you think you hear an interval that is a minor second, you should make a tally mark on the paper. After each minor second on this tape, following a brief pause, a high electronic tone will be heard. If the electronic tone is heard after you make a tally mark, you will know that the response was correct. If you have made a mark and failed to hear the tone, you will know you made an error. It is, of course, also an error to fail to make a mark when a minor second is heard.

The first interval heard on each tape is the interval to be discriminated. If you forget the sound of it, you will be reminded every time you hear an interval followed by the electronic tone. Soon you will become skillful in detecting the difference between this interval and the others on the tape. Think of the task as trying to make a tally mark just before each electronic sound, and only then.

These instructions sound complex, but the process will become clear as soon as the tape is begun.

Make the tally marks in a row until a mistake is made. Then start a new line below. Try to make 15 correct marks in a row. As soon as you do this, go on to the next lesson, even if the tape is not finished. If necessary, rewind the tape to accomplish this goal.

SERIES A6

HARMONIC INTERVAL DICTATION

The purpose of this series is to develop the ability to write the upper of two notes that form harmonic intervals that you hear. A printed worksheet and tape recording are provided for each lesson.

For each interval on the worksheet, there is a large note that is the lower of the two notes that make up the interval. Write the upper note after you hear the interval on the tape. To the right, two smaller notes indicate the correct answer. To do a lesson, place a shield over the smaller notes to the right. Listen to the tape, write the note that will complete the interval you heard, and only then slide the shield to the right to find the correct answer. You may stop the tape occasionally if you need more time. Be sure to make a committed response before looking at the right answer. Learning is much more effective when this is done. Your response is correct if the note you have written is the same as the small note, or if it is enharmonic with it.

A6-1 Harmonic interval dictation: major and minor seconds

(COPY 1)

A6-1 Harmonic interval dictation: major and minor seconds

(COPY 2)

A6-1 Harmonic interval dictation: major and minor seconds

(COPY 3)

A6-2 Harmonic interval dictation: major and minor thirds

(COPY 1)

A6-2 Harmonic interval dictation: major and minor thirds

(COPY 2)

A6-2 Harmonic interval dictation: major and minor thirds
(COPY 3)

A6-3 Harmonic interval dictation: perfect and augmented fourths, perfect and diminished fifths

(COPY 1)

A6-3 Harmonic interval dictation: perfect and augmented fourths, perfect and diminished fifths

(COPY 2)

A6-3 Harmonic interval dictation: perfect and augmented fourths, perfect and diminished fifths

(COPY 3)

A6-4 Harmonic interval dictation: major and minor sixths

(COPY 1)

A6-4 Harmonic interval dictation: major and minor sixths

(COPY 2)

A6-4 Harmonic interval dictation: major and minor sixths

(COPY 3)

A6-5 Harmonic interval dictation: major and minor sevenths, perfect octaves

(COPY 1)

A6-5 Harmonic interval dictation: major and minor sevenths, perfect octaves

(COPY 2)

A6-5 Harmonic interval dictation: major and minor sevenths, perfect octaves

(COPY 3)

A6-6 Harmonic interval dictation: all intervals previously studied

(COPY 1)

A6-6 Harmonic interval dictation: all intervals previously studied

(COPY 2)

A6-6 Harmonic interval dictation: all intervals previously studied

(COPY 3)

A6-7 Harmonic interval dictation: all intervals previous studied
(COPY 1)

A6-7 Harmonic interval dictation: all intervals previous studied

(COPY 2)

A6-7 Harmonic interval dictation: all intervals previous studied

(COPY 3)

SERIES A7

HARMONIC INTERVAL IDENTIFICATION

The purpose of this series is to develop the ability to identify harmonic intervals formed by two tones that you hear. The following set of symbols will be used to identify the intervals:

m2	minor second	P5	perfect fifth
M2	major second	m6	minor sixth
m3	minor third	M6	major sixth
M3	major third	m7	minor seventh
P4	perfect fourth	M7	major seventh
T	tritone	P8	perfect octave

A printed worksheet and a tape recording are provided for each lesson. On the worksheet, you should work across the page following each number. Use a shield to cover the correct answer until you have heard the interval on the tape and have written your answer. Move the shield to the right to find the correct answer, and then move on to the next interval to the right. You may stop the tape occasionally if you need more time.

A7-1 Harmonic interval identification: major and minor seconds
(COPY 1)

1	____ m2	____ M2	____ M2	____ m2	____ m2	____ M2	____ m2	____ M2
2	____ m2	____ M2	____ M2	____ m2	____ M2	____ m2	____ m2	____ M2
3	____ m2	____ M2	____ M2	____ m2	____ M2	____ m2	____ m2	____ M2
4	____ M2	____ m2	____ m2	____ M2	____ M2	____ m2	____ m2	____ M2
5	____ m2	____ M2	____ M2	____ m2	____ m2	____ M2	____ m2	____ M2
6	____ M2	____ m2	____ m2	____ M2	____ M2	____ m2	____ m2	____ M2
7	____ M2	____ m2	____ m2	____ M2	____ m2	____ m2	____ M2	____ M2
8	____ M2	____ m2	____ m2	____ m2	____ m2	____ M2	____ M2	____ M2
9	____ m2	____ m2	____ M2	____ m2	____ m2	____ M2	____ M2	____ m2
10	____ m2	____ M2	____ M2	____ m2	____ M2	____ M2	____ m2	____ m2
11	____ M2	____ m2	____ M2	____ m2	____ m2	____ M2	____ m2	____ M2
12	____ m2	____ M2	____ M2	____ m2	____ m2	____ m2	____ M2	____ M2

A7-1 Harmonic interval identification: major and minor seconds
(COPY 2)

1	____ m2	____ M2	____ M2	____ m2	____ m2	____ M2	____ m2	____ M2
2	____ m2	____ M2	____ M2	____ m2	____ M2	____ m2	____ m2	____ M2
3	____ m2	____ M2	____ M2	____ m2	____ M2	____ m2	____ m2	____ M2
4	____ M2	____ m2	____ m2	____ M2	____ M2	____ m2	____ m2	____ M2
5	____ m2	____ M2	____ M2	____ m2	____ m2	____ M2	____ m2	____ M2
6	____ M2	____ m2	____ m2	____ M2	____ M2	____ m2	____ m2	____ M2
7	____ M2	____ m2	____ m2	____ M2	____ m2	____ m2	____ M2	____ M2
8	____ M2	____ m2	____ m2	____ m2	____ m2	____ M2	____ M2	____ M2
9	____ m2	____ m2	____ M2	____ m2	____ m2	____ M2	____ M2	____ m2
10	____ m2	____ M2	____ M2	____ m2	____ M2	____ M2	____ m2	____ m2
11	____ M2	____ m2	____ M2	____ m2	____ m2	____ M2	____ m2	____ M2
12	____ m2	____ M2	____ M2	____ m2	____ m2	____ m2	____ M2	____ M2

A7-I Harmonic interval identification: major and minor seconds
(COPY 3)

1 ____ m2 ____ M2 ____ M2 ____ m2 ____ m2 ____ M2 ____ m2 ____ M2
2 ____ m2 ____ M2 ____ M2 ____ m2 ____ M2 ____ m2 ____ m2 ____ M2
3 ____ m2 ____ M2 ____ M2 ____ m2 ____ M2 ____ m2 ____ m2 ____ M2
4 ____ M2 ____ m2 ____ m2 ____ M2 ____ M2 ____ m2 ____ m2 ____ M2
5 ____ m2 ____ M2 ____ M2 ____ m2 ____ m2 ____ M2 ____ m2 ____ M2
6 ____ M2 ____ m2 ____ m2 ____ M2 ____ M2 ____ m2 ____ m2 ____ M2
7 ____ M2 ____ m2 ____ m2 ____ M2 ____ m2 ____ m2 ____ M2 ____ M2
8 ____ M2 ____ m2 ____ m2 ____ m2 ____ m2 ____ M2 ____ M2 ____ M2
9 ____ m2 ____ m2 ____ M2 ____ m2 ____ m2 ____ M2 ____ M2 ____ m2
10 ____ m2 ____ M2 ____ M2 ____ m2 ____ M2 ____ M2 ____ m2 ____ m2
11 ____ M2 ____ m2 ____ M2 ____ m2 ____ m2 ____ M2 ____ m2 ____ M2
12 ____ m2 ____ M2 ____ M2 ____ m2 ____ m2 ____ m2 ____ M2 ____ M2

A7-I Harmonic interval identification: major and minor seconds
(COPY 4)

1 ____ m2 ____ M2 ____ M2 ____ m2 ____ m2 ____ M2 ____ m2 ____ M2
2 ____ m2 ____ M2 ____ M2 ____ m2 ____ M2 ____ m2 ____ m2 ____ M2
3 ____ m2 ____ M2 ____ M2 ____ m2 ____ M2 ____ m2 ____ m2 ____ M2
4 ____ M2 ____ m2 ____ m2 ____ M2 ____ M2 ____ m2 ____ m2 ____ M2
5 ____ m2 ____ M2 ____ M2 ____ m2 ____ m2 ____ M2 ____ m2 ____ M2
6 ____ M2 ____ m2 ____ m2 ____ M2 ____ M2 ____ m2 ____ m2 ____ M2
7 ____ M2 ____ m2 ____ m2 ____ M2 ____ m2 ____ m2 ____ M2 ____ M2
8 ____ M2 ____ m2 ____ m2 ____ m2 ____ m2 ____ M2 ____ M2 ____ M2
9 ____ m2 ____ m2 ____ M2 ____ m2 ____ m2 ____ M2 ____ M2 ____ m2
10 ____ m2 ____ M2 ____ M2 ____ m2 ____ M2 ____ M2 ____ m2 ____ m2
11 ____ M2 ____ m2 ____ M2 ____ m2 ____ m2 ____ M2 ____ m2 ____ M2
12 ____ m2 ____ M2 ____ M2 ____ m2 ____ m2 ____ m2 ____ M2 ____ M2

A7-2 Harmonic interval identification: major and minor thirds
(COPY 1)

1 ____ M3 ____ m3 ____ M3 ____ m3 ____ m3 ____ M3 ____ m3 ____ M3

2 ____ M3 ____ m3 ____ m3 ____ M3 ____ M3 ____ m3 ____ m3 ____ M3

3 ____ M3 ____ m3 ____ m3 ____ M3 ____ m3 ____ M3 ____ m3 ____ m3

4 ____ m3 ____ M3 ____ M3 ____ m3 ____ m3 ____ M3 ____ m3 ____ m3

5 ____ M3 ____ m3 ____ m3 ____ M3 ____ m3 ____ M3 ____ m3 ____ M3

6 ____ m3 ____ M3 ____ M3 ____ m3 ____ M3 ____ m3 ____ M3 ____ M3

7 ____ M3 ____ m3 ____ M3 ____ M3 ____ m3 ____ M3 ____ m3 ____ m3

8 ____ M3 ____ m3 ____ M3 ____ m3 ____ M3 ____ m3 ____ M3 ____ m3

9 ____ m3 ____ m3 ____ M3 ____ m3 ____ M3 ____ m3 ____ m3 ____ m3

10 ____ M3 ____ m3 ____ M3 ____ M3 ____ m3 ____ M3 ____ m3 ____ m3

11 ____ m3 ____ m3 ____ m3 ____ m3 ____ M3 ____ m3 ____ m3 ____ M3

12 ____ m3 ____ M3 ____ m3 ____ m3 ____ M3 ____ m3 ____ M3 ____ M3

A7-2 Harmonic interval identification: major and minor thirds
(COPY 2)

1 ____ M3 ____ m3 ____ M3 ____ m3 ____ m3 ____ M3 ____ m3 ____ M3

2 ____ M3 ____ m3 ____ m3 ____ M3 ____ M3 ____ m3 ____ m3 ____ M3

3 ____ M3 ____ m3 ____ m3 ____ M3 ____ m3 ____ M3 ____ m3 ____ m3

4 ____ m3 ____ M3 ____ M3 ____ m3 ____ m3 ____ M3 ____ m3 ____ m3

5 ____ M3 ____ m3 ____ m3 ____ M3 ____ m3 ____ M3 ____ m3 ____ M3

6 ____ m3 ____ M3 ____ M3 ____ m3 ____ M3 ____ m3 ____ M3 ____ M3

7 ____ M3 ____ m3 ____ M3 ____ M3 ____ m3 ____ M3 ____ m3 ____ m3

8 ____ M3 ____ m3 ____ M3 ____ m3 ____ M3 ____ m3 ____ M3 ____ m3

9 ____ m3 ____ m3 ____ M3 ____ m3 ____ M3 ____ m3 ____ m3 ____ m3

10 ____ M3 ____ m3 ____ M3 ____ M3 ____ m3 ____ M3 ____ m3 ____ m3

11 ____ m3 ____ m3 ____ m3 ____ m3 ____ M3 ____ m3 ____ m3 ____ M3

12 ____ m3 ____ M3 ____ m3 ____ m3 ____ M3 ____ m3 ____ M3 ____ M3

A7-2 Harmonic interval identification: major and minor thirds
(COPY 3)

1 ____ M3 ____ m3 ____ M3 ____ m3 ____ m3 ____ M3 ____ m3 ____ M3

2 ____ M3 ____ m3 ____ m3 ____ M3 ____ M3 ____ m3 ____ m3 ____ M3

3 ____ M3 ____ m3 ____ m3 ____ M3 ____ m3 ____ M3 ____ m3 ____ m3

4 ____ m3 ____ M3 ____ M3 ____ m3 ____ m3 ____ M3 ____ m3 ____ m3

5 ____ M3 ____ m3 ____ m3 ____ M3 ____ m3 ____ M3 ____ m3 ____ M3

6 ____ m3 ____ M3 ____ M3 ____ m3 ____ M3 ____ m3 ____ M3 ____ M3

7 ____ M3 ____ m3 ____ M3 ____ M3 ____ m3 ____ M3 ____ m3 ____ m3

8 ____ M3 ____ m3 ____ M3 ____ m3 ____ M3 ____ m3 ____ M3 ____ m3

9 ____ m3 ____ m3 ____ M3 ____ m3 ____ M3 ____ m3 ____ m3 ____ m3

10 ____ M3 ____ m3 ____ M3 ____ M3 ____ m3 ____ M3 ____ m3 ____ m3

11 ____ m3 ____ m3 ____ m3 ____ m3 ____ M3 ____ m3 ____ m3 ____ M3

12 ____ m3 ____ M3 ____ m3 ____ m3 ____ M3 ____ m3 ____ M3 ____ M3

A7-2 Harmonic interval identification: major and minor thirds
(COPY 4)

1 ____ M3 ____ m3 ____ M3 ____ m3 ____ m3 ____ M3 ____ m3 ____ M3

2 ____ M3 ____ m3 ____ m3 ____ M3 ____ M3 ____ m3 ____ m3 ____ M3

3 ____ M3 ____ m3 ____ m3 ____ M3 ____ m3 ____ M3 ____ m3 ____ m3

4 ____ m3 ____ M3 ____ M3 ____ m3 ____ m3 ____ M3 ____ m3 ____ m3

5 ____ M3 ____ m3 ____ m3 ____ M3 ____ m3 ____ M3 ____ m3 ____ M3

6 ____ m3 ____ M3 ____ M3 ____ m3 ____ M3 ____ m3 ____ M3 ____ M3

7 ____ M3 ____ m3 ____ M3 ____ M3 ____ m3 ____ M3 ____ m3 ____ m3

8 ____ M3 ____ m3 ____ M3 ____ m3 ____ M3 ____ m3 ____ M3 ____ m3

9 ____ m3 ____ m3 ____ M3 ____ m3 ____ M3 ____ m3 ____ m3 ____ m3

10 ____ M3 ____ m3 ____ M3 ____ M3 ____ m3 ____ M3 ____ m3 ____ m3

11 ____ m3 ____ m3 ____ m3 ____ m3 ____ M3 ____ m3 ____ m3 ____ M3

12 ____ m3 ____ M3 ____ m3 ____ m3 ____ M3 ____ m3 ____ M3 ____ M3

A7-3 Harmonic interval identification: perfect fourths and fifths
(COPY 1)

1 ____ P5 ____ P4 ____ P5 ____ P4 ____ P4 ____ P5 ____ P4 ____ P5
2 ____ P4 ____ P5 ____ P4 ____ P5 ____ P4 ____ P5 ____ P4 ____ P5
3 ____ P5 ____ P4 ____ P5 ____ P4 ____ P5 ____ P4 ____ P5 ____ P4
4 ____ P5 ____ P4 ____ P5 ____ P5 ____ P4 ____ P5 ____ P4 ____ P5
5 ____ P5 ____ P5 ____ P4 ____ P4 ____ P4 ____ P4 ____ P5 ____ P5
6 ____ P4 ____ P5 ____ P5 ____ P4 ____ P5 ____ P4 ____ P5 ____ P4
7 ____ P5 ____ P5 ____ P4 ____ P5 ____ P5 ____ P5 ____ P4 ____ P4
8 ____ P5 ____ P4 ____ P5 ____ P5 ____ P4 ____ P4 ____ P5 ____ P5
9 ____ P4 ____ P4 ____ P5 ____ P4 ____ P5 ____ P4 ____ P4 ____ P4
10 ____ P5 ____ P4 ____ P4 ____ P5 ____ P5 ____ P4 ____ P4 ____ P5
11 ____ P5 ____ P5 ____ P4 ____ P4 ____ P5 ____ P4 ____ P5 ____ P4
12 ____ P4 ____ P5 ____ P4 ____ P5 ____ P4 ____ P5 ____ P5 ____ P4

A7-3 Harmonic interval identification: perfect fourths and fifths
(COPY 2)

1 ____ P5 ____ P4 ____ P5 ____ P4 ____ P4 ____ P5 ____ P4 ____ P5
2 ____ P4 ____ P5 ____ P4 ____ P5 ____ P4 ____ P5 ____ P4 ____ P5
3 ____ P5 ____ P4 ____ P5 ____ P4 ____ P5 ____ P4 ____ P5 ____ P4
4 ____ P5 ____ P4 ____ P5 ____ P5 ____ P4 ____ P5 ____ P4 ____ P5
5 ____ P5 ____ P5 ____ P4 ____ P4 ____ P4 ____ P4 ____ P5 ____ P5
6 ____ P4 ____ P5 ____ P5 ____ P4 ____ P5 ____ P4 ____ P5 ____ P4
7 ____ P5 ____ P5 ____ P4 ____ P5 ____ P5 ____ P5 ____ P4 ____ P4
8 ____ P5 ____ P4 ____ P5 ____ P5 ____ P4 ____ P4 ____ P5 ____ P5
9 ____ P4 ____ P4 ____ P5 ____ P4 ____ P5 ____ P4 ____ P4 ____ P4
10 ____ P5 ____ P4 ____ P4 ____ P5 ____ P5 ____ P4 ____ P4 ____ P5
11 ____ P5 ____ P5 ____ P4 ____ P4 ____ P5 ____ P4 ____ P5 ____ P4
12 ____ P4 ____ P5 ____ P4 ____ P5 ____ P4 ____ P5 ____ P5 ____ P4

A7-3 Harmonic interval identification: perfect fourths and fifths
(COPY 3)

1 ____ P5 ____ P4 ____ P5 ____ P4 ____ P4 ____ P5 ____ P4 ____ P5

2 ____ P4 ____ P5 ____ P4 ____ P5 ____ P4 ____ P5 ____ P4 ____ P5

3 ____ P5 ____ P4 ____ P5 ____ P4 ____ P5 ____ P4 ____ P5 ____ P4

4 ____ P5 ____ P4 ____ P5 ____ P5 ____ P4 ____ P5 ____ P4 ____ P5

5 ____ P5 ____ P5 ____ P4 ____ P4 ____ P4 ____ P4 ____ P5 ____ P5

6 ____ P4 ____ P5 ____ P5 ____ P4 ____ P5 ____ P4 ____ P5 ____ P4

7 ____ P5 ____ P5 ____ P4 ____ P5 ____ P5 ____ P5 ____ P4 ____ P4

8 ____ P5 ____ P4 ____ P5 ____ P5 ____ P4 ____ P4 ____ P5 ____ P5

9 ____ P4 ____ P4 ____ P5 ____ P4 ____ P5 ____ P4 ____ P4 ____ P4

10 ____ P5 ____ P4 ____ P4 ____ P5 ____ P5 ____ P4 ____ P4 ____ P5

11 ____ P5 ____ P5 ____ P4 ____ P4 ____ P5 ____ P4 ____ P5 ____ P4

12 ____ P4 ____ P5 ____ P4 ____ P5 ____ P4 ____ P5 ____ P5 ____ P4

A7-3 Harmonic interval identification: perfect fourths and fifths
(COPY 4)

1 ____ P5 ____ P4 ____ P5 ____ P4 ____ P4 ____ P5 ____ P4 ____ P5

2 ____ P4 ____ P5 ____ P4 ____ P5 ____ P4 ____ P5 ____ P4 ____ P5

3 ____ P5 ____ P4 ____ P5 ____ P4 ____ P5 ____ P4 ____ P5 ____ P4

4 ____ P5 ____ P4 ____ P5 ____ P5 ____ P4 ____ P5 ____ P4 ____ P5

5 ____ P5 ____ P5 ____ P4 ____ P4 ____ P4 ____ P4 ____ P5 ____ P5

6 ____ P4 ____ P5 ____ P5 ____ P4 ____ P5 ____ P4 ____ P5 ____ P4

7 ____ P5 ____ P5 ____ P4 ____ P5 ____ P5 ____ P5 ____ P4 ____ P4

8 ____ P5 ____ P4 ____ P5 ____ P5 ____ P4 ____ P4 ____ P5 ____ P5

9 ____ P4 ____ P4 ____ P5 ____ P4 ____ P5 ____ P4 ____ P4 ____ P4

10 ____ P5 ____ P4 ____ P4 ____ P5 ____ P5 ____ P4 ____ P4 ____ P5

11 ____ P5 ____ P5 ____ P4 ____ P4 ____ P5 ____ P4 ____ P5 ____ P4

12 ____ P4 ____ P5 ____ P4 ____ P5 ____ P4 ____ P5 ____ P5 ____ P4

A7-4 Harmonic interval identification: major and minor sixths
(COPY 1)

1	____ M6	____ m6	____ m6	____ M6	____ M6	____ m6	____ m6	____ M6
2	____ M6	____ m6	____ M6	____ m6	____ m6	____ M6	____ m6	____ M6
3	____ m6	____ M6	____ M6	____ m6	____ M6	____ m6	____ m6	____ M6
4	____ m6	____ M6	____ M6	____ m6	____ M6	____ m6	____ m6	____ M6
5	____ m6	____ M6	____ M6	____ m6	____ m6	____ m6	____ M6	____ M6
6	____ M6	____ m6	____ m6	____ M6	____ M6	____ m6	____ m6	____ M6
7	____ m6	____ m6	____ M6	____ M6	____ M6	____ M6	____ m6	____ m6
8	____ M6	____ m6	____ M6	____ M6	____ m6	____ m6	____ m6	____ M6
9	____ m6	____ M6	____ m6	____ M6	____ m6	____ M6	____ M6	____ M6
10	____ M6	____ m6	____ M6	____ M6	____ m6	____ M6	____ M6	____ m6
11	____ M6	____ M6	____ m6	____ m6	____ M6	____ m6	____ M6	____ m6
12	____ M6	____ M6	____ m6	____ m6	____ m6	____ M6	____ M6	____ m6

A7-4 Harmonic interval identification: major and minor sixths
(COPY 2)

1	____ M6	____ m6	____ m6	____ M6	____ M6	____ m6	____ m6	____ M6
2	____ M6	____ m6	____ M6	____ m6	____ m6	____ M6	____ m6	____ M6
3	____ m6	____ M6	____ M6	____ m6	____ M6	____ m6	____ m6	____ M6
4	____ m6	____ M6	____ M6	____ m6	____ M6	____ m6	____ m6	____ M6
5	____ m6	____ M6	____ M6	____ m6	____ m6	____ m6	____ M6	____ M6
6	____ M6	____ m6	____ m6	____ M6	____ M6	____ m6	____ m6	____ M6
7	____ m6	____ m6	____ M6	____ M6	____ M6	____ M6	____ m6	____ m6
8	____ M6	____ m6	____ M6	____ M6	____ m6	____ m6	____ m6	____ M6
9	____ m6	____ M6	____ m6	____ M6	____ m6	____ M6	____ M6	____ M6
10	____ M6	____ m6	____ M6	____ M6	____ m6	____ M6	____ M6	____ m6
11	____ M6	____ M6	____ m6	____ m6	____ M6	____ m6	____ M6	____ m6
12	____ M6	____ M6	____ m6	____ m6	____ m6	____ M6	____ M6	____ m6

A7-4 Harmonic interval identification: major and minor sixths
(COPY 3)

1	____ M6	____ m6	____ m6	____ M6	____ M6	____ m6	____ m6	____ M6
2	____ M6	____ m6	____ M6	____ m6	____ m6	____ M6	____ m6	____ M6
3	____ m6	____ M6	____ M6	____ m6	____ M6	____ m6	____ m6	____ M6
4	____ m6	____ M6	____ M6	____ m6	____ M6	____ m6	____ m6	____ M6
5	____ m6	____ M6	____ M6	____ m6	____ m6	____ m6	____ M6	____ M6
6	____ M6	____ m6	____ m6	____ M6	____ M6	____ m6	____ m6	____ M6
7	____ m6	____ m6	____ M6	____ M6	____ M6	____ M6	____ m6	____ m6
8	____ M6	____ m6	____ M6	____ M6	____ m6	____ m6	____ m6	____ M6
9	____ m6	____ M6	____ m6	____ M6	____ m6	____ M6	____ M6	____ M6
10	____ M6	____ m6	____ M6	____ M6	____ m6	____ M6	____ M6	____ m6
11	____ M6	____ M6	____ m6	____ m6	____ M6	____ m6	____ M6	____ m6
12	____ M6	____ M6	____ m6	____ m6	____ m6	____ M6	____ M6	____ m6

A7-4 Harmonic interval identification: major and minor sixths
(COPY 4)

1	____ M6	____ m6	____ m6	____ M6	____ M6	____ m6	____ m6	____ M6
2	____ M6	____ m6	____ M6	____ m6	____ m6	____ M6	____ m6	____ M6
3	____ m6	____ M6	____ M6	____ m6	____ M6	____ m6	____ m6	____ M6
4	____ m6	____ M6	____ M6	____ m6	____ M6	____ m6	____ m6	____ M6
5	____ m6	____ M6	____ M6	____ m6	____ m6	____ m6	____ M6	____ M6
6	____ M6	____ m6	____ m6	____ M6	____ M6	____ m6	____ m6	____ M6
7	____ m6	____ m6	____ M6	____ M6	____ M6	____ M6	____ m6	____ m6
8	____ M6	____ m6	____ M6	____ M6	____ m6	____ m6	____ m6	____ M6
9	____ m6	____ M6	____ m6	____ M6	____ m6	____ M6	____ M6	____ M6
10	____ M6	____ m6	____ M6	____ M6	____ m6	____ M6	____ M6	____ m6
11	____ M6	____ M6	____ m6	____ m6	____ M6	____ m6	____ M6	____ m6
12	____ M6	____ M6	____ m6	____ m6	____ m6	____ M6	____ M6	____ m6

A7-5 Harmonic interval identification: tritones, major and minor sevenths, perfect octaves

(COPY 1)

1	____ P8	____ M7	____ m7	____ P8	____ m7	____ M7	____ T	____ m7
2	____ m7	____ M7	____ M7	____ m7	____ m7	____ M7	____ T	____ T
3	____ T	____ M7	____ m7	____ P8	____ T	____ M7	____ P8	____ m7
4	____ P8	____ M7	____ T	____ m7	____ m7	____ M7	____ T	____ m7
5	____ M7	____ m7	____ T	____ M7	____ m7	____ M7	____ P8	____ T
6	____ P8	____ M7	____ m7	____ T	____ m7	____ M7	____ M7	____ T
7	____ M7	____ T	____ m7	____ m7	____ T	____ M7	____ M7	____ m7
8	____ M7	____ m7	____ T	____ m7	____ T	____ M7	____ T	____ M7
9	____ m7	____ M7	____ T	____ m7	____ T	____ M7	____ m7	____ m7
10	____ M7	____ m7	____ M7	____ M7	____ m7	____ m7	____ m7	____ M7
11	____ m7	____ M7	____ m7	____ m7	____ m7	____ M7	____ m7	____ m7
12	____ M7	____ m7	____ m7	____ M7	____ M7	____ m7	____ M7	____ M7

A7-5 Harmonic interval identification: tritones, major and minor sevenths, perfect octaves

(COPY 2)

1	____ P8	____ M7	____ m7	____ P8	____ m7	____ M7	____ T	____ m7
2	____ m7	____ M7	____ M7	____ m7	____ m7	____ M7	____ T	____ T
3	____ T	____ M7	____ m7	____ P8	____ T	____ M7	____ P8	____ m7
4	____ P8	____ M7	____ T	____ m7	____ m7	____ M7	____ T	____ m7
5	____ M7	____ m7	____ T	____ M7	____ m7	____ M7	____ P8	____ T
6	____ P8	____ M7	____ m7	____ T	____ m7	____ M7	____ M7	____ T
7	____ M7	____ T	____ m7	____ m7	____ T	____ M7	____ M7	____ m7
8	____ M7	____ m7	____ T	____ m7	____ T	____ M7	____ T	____ M7
9	____ m7	____ M7	____ T	____ m7	____ T	____ M7	____ m7	____ m7
10	____ M7	____ m7	____ M7	____ M7	____ m7	____ m7	____ m7	____ M7
11	____ m7	____ M7	____ m7	____ m7	____ m7	____ M7	____ m7	____ m7
12	____ M7	____ m7	____ m7	____ M7	____ M7	____ m7	____ M7	____ M7

A7-5 Harmonic interval identification: tritones, major and minor sevenths, perfect octaves

(COPY 3)

1 ____ P8 ____ M7 ____ m7 ____ P8 ____ m7 ____ M7 ____ T ____ m7

2 ____ m7 ____ M7 ____ M7 ____ m7 ____ m7 ____ M7 ____ T ____ T

3 ____ T ____ M7 ____ m7 ____ P8 ____ T ____ M7 ____ P8 ____ m7

4 ____ P8 ____ M7 ____ T ____ m7 ____ m7 ____ M7 ____ T ____ m7

5 ____ M7 ____ m7 ____ T ____ M7 ____ m7 ____ M7 ____ P8 ____ T

6 ____ P8 ____ M7 ____ m7 ____ T ____ m7 ____ M7 ____ M7 ____ T

7 ____ M7 ____ T ____ m7 ____ m7 ____ T ____ M7 ____ M7 ____ m7

8 ____ M7 ____ m7 ____ T ____ m7 ____ T ____ M7 ____ T ____ M7

9 ____ m7 ____ M7 ____ T ____ m7 ____ T ____ M7 ____ m7 ____ m7

10 ____ M7 ____ m7 ____ M7 ____ M7 ____ m7 ____ m7 ____ m7 ____ M7

11 ____ m7 ____ M7 ____ m7 ____ m7 ____ m7 ____ M7 ____ m7 ____ m7

12 ____ M7 ____ m7 ____ m7 ____ M7 ____ M7 ____ m7 ____ M7 ____ M7

A7-5 Harmonic interval identification: tritones, major and minor sevenths, perfect octaves

(COPY 4)

1 ____ P8 ____ M7 ____ m7 ____ P8 ____ m7 ____ M7 ____ T ____ m7

2 ____ m7 ____ M7 ____ M7 ____ m7 ____ m7 ____ M7 ____ T ____ T

3 ____ T ____ M7 ____ m7 ____ P8 ____ T ____ M7 ____ P8 ____ m7

4 ____ P8 ____ M7 ____ T ____ m7 ____ m7 ____ M7 ____ T ____ m7

5 ____ M7 ____ m7 ____ T ____ M7 ____ m7 ____ M7 ____ P8 ____ T

6 ____ P8 ____ M7 ____ m7 ____ T ____ m7 ____ M7 ____ M7 ____ T

7 ____ M7 ____ T ____ m7 ____ m7 ____ T ____ M7 ____ M7 ____ m7

8 ____ M7 ____ m7 ____ T ____ m7 ____ T ____ M7 ____ T ____ M7

9 ____ m7 ____ M7 ____ T ____ m7 ____ T ____ M7 ____ m7 ____ m7

10 ____ M7 ____ m7 ____ M7 ____ M7 ____ m7 ____ m7 ____ m7 ____ M7

11 ____ m7 ____ M7 ____ m7 ____ m7 ____ m7 ____ M7 ____ m7 ____ m7

12 ____ M7 ____ m7 ____ m7 ____ M7 ____ M7 ____ m7 ____ M7 ____ M7

A7-6
(COPY 1)

Harmonic interval identification: major and minor thirds, major and minor sixths

1	___ M3	___ m3	___ M6	___ m6	___ m6	___ M6	___ M3	___ m3
2	___ m3	___ M3	___ M6	___ m6	___ m6	___ m3	___ M3	___ M6
3	___ m3	___ M6	___ m6	___ M3	___ M3	___ m6	___ m3	___ M6
4	___ M6	___ M3	___ m6	___ m3	___ m6	___ m3	___ M3	___ M6
5	___ m3	___ M6	___ M3	___ m6	___ M3	___ m6	___ m3	___ M6
6	___ M6	___ M3	___ m6	___ m3	___ M3	___ m6	___ m3	___ M6
7	___ M6	___ m3	___ m6	___ M3	___ m6	___ M3	___ m3	___ M6
8	___ m3	___ M6	___ M3	___ M3	___ M6	___ m6	___ m3	___ M6
9	___ m6	___ M3	___ M6	___ M3	___ m6	___ m3	___ M6	___ M6
10	___ M3	___ m6	___ m6	___ M3	___ m3	___ M6	___ M6	___ M3
11	___ M6	___ M3	___ m6	___ m3	___ M6	___ m6	___ m3	___ M3
12	___ M6	___ m3	___ M6	___ m3	___ M3	___ M3	___ M6	___ m6

A7-6
(COPY 2)

Harmonic interval identification: major and minor thirds, major and minor sixths

1	___ M3	___ m3	___ M6	___ m6	___ m6	___ M6	___ M3	___ m3
2	___ m3	___ M3	___ M6	___ m6	___ m6	___ m3	___ M3	___ M6
3	___ m3	___ M6	___ m6	___ M3	___ M3	___ m6	___ m3	___ M6
4	___ M6	___ M3	___ m6	___ m3	___ m6	___ m3	___ M3	___ M6
5	___ m3	___ M6	___ M3	___ m6	___ M3	___ m6	___ m3	___ M6
6	___ M6	___ M3	___ m6	___ m3	___ M3	___ m6	___ m3	___ M6
7	___ M6	___ m3	___ m6	___ M3	___ m6	___ M3	___ m3	___ M6
8	___ m3	___ M6	___ M3	___ M3	___ M6	___ m6	___ m3	___ M6
9	___ m6	___ M3	___ M6	___ M3	___ m6	___ m3	___ M6	___ M6
10	___ M3	___ m6	___ m6	___ M3	___ m3	___ M6	___ M6	___ M3
11	___ M6	___ M3	___ m6	___ m3	___ M6	___ m6	___ m3	___ M3
12	___ M6	___ m3	___ M6	___ m3	___ M3	___ M3	___ M6	___ m6

A7-6 (COPY 3) Harmonic interval identification: major and minor thirds, major and minor sixths

1	____ M3	____ m3	____ M6	____ m6	____ m6	____ M6	____ M3	____ m3
2	____ m3	____ M3	____ M6	____ m6	____ m6	____ m3	____ M3	____ M6
3	____ m3	____ M6	____ m6	____ M3	____ M3	____ m6	____ m3	____ M6
4	____ M6	____ M3	____ m6	____ m3	____ m6	____ m3	____ M3	____ M6
5	____ m3	____ M6	____ M3	____ m6	____ M3	____ m6	____ m3	____ M6
6	____ M6	____ M3	____ m6	____ m3	____ M3	____ m6	____ m3	____ M6
7	____ M6	____ m3	____ m6	____ M3	____ m6	____ M3	____ m3	____ M6
8	____ m3	____ M6	____ M3	____ M3	____ M6	____ m6	____ m3	____ M6
9	____ m6	____ M3	____ M6	____ M3	____ m6	____ m3	____ M6	____ M6
10	____ M3	____ m6	____ m6	____ M3	____ m3	____ M6	____ M6	____ M3
11	____ M6	____ M3	____ m6	____ m3	____ M6	____ m6	____ m3	____ M3
12	____ M6	____ m3	____ M6	____ m3	____ M3	____ M3	____ M6	____ m6

A7-6 (COPY 4) Harmonic interval identification: major and minor thirds, major and minor sixths

1	____ M3	____ m3	____ M6	____ m6	____ m6	____ M6	____ M3	____ m3
2	____ m3	____ M3	____ M6	____ m6	____ m6	____ m3	____ M3	____ M6
3	____ m3	____ M6	____ m6	____ M3	____ M3	____ m6	____ m3	____ M6
4	____ M6	____ M3	____ m6	____ m3	____ m6	____ m3	____ M3	____ M6
5	____ m3	____ M6	____ M3	____ m6	____ M3	____ m6	____ m3	____ M6
6	____ M6	____ M3	____ m6	____ m3	____ M3	____ m6	____ m3	____ M6
7	____ M6	____ m3	____ m6	____ M3	____ m6	____ M3	____ m3	____ M6
8	____ m3	____ M6	____ M3	____ M3	____ M6	____ m6	____ m3	____ M6
9	____ m6	____ M3	____ M6	____ M3	____ m6	____ m3	____ M6	____ M6
10	____ M3	____ m6	____ m6	____ M3	____ m3	____ M6	____ M6	____ M3
11	____ M6	____ M3	____ m6	____ m3	____ M6	____ m6	____ m3	____ M3
12	____ M6	____ m3	____ M6	____ m3	____ M3	____ M3	____ M6	____ m6

A7-7 (COPY 1) Harmonic interval identification: major and minor seconds, tritones, major and minor sevenths

1 ____ m2 ____ M2 ____ m7 ____ M7 ____ T ____ m2 ____ m7 ____ T
2 ____ M7 ____ m7 ____ M2 ____ m2 ____ M7 ____ m7 ____ T ____ M2
3 ____ M2 ____ m2 ____ m2 ____ M2 ____ M7 ____ m7 ____ T ____ M7
4 ____ m7 ____ M2 ____ M7 ____ m2 ____ m2 ____ M7 ____ M2 ____ m7
5 ____ m7 ____ M2 ____ M7 ____ m2 ____ M7 ____ m2 ____ M2 ____ m7
6 ____ T ____ m7 ____ m7 ____ M2 ____ M2 ____ m7 ____ M7 ____ m2
7 ____ M7 ____ m2 ____ m2 ____ M7 ____ T ____ m7 ____ T ____ M7
8 ____ m7 ____ M2 ____ M7 ____ m2 ____ M7 ____ m2 ____ m7 ____ M2
9 ____ T ____ m7 ____ T ____ m7 ____ M7 ____ m2 ____ M2 ____ m7
10 ____ T ____ m7 ____ M7 ____ m2 ____ M2 ____ M7 ____ M7 ____ m7
11 ____ T ____ M7 ____ m7 ____ M7 ____ m2 ____ T ____ m7 ____ M7
12 ____ m2 ____ m7 ____ T ____ m7 ____ m7 ____ M7 ____ m2 ____ M7

A7-7 (COPY 2) Harmonic interval identification: major and minor seconds, tritones, major and minor sevenths

1 ____ m2 ____ M2 ____ m7 ____ M7 ____ T ____ m2 ____ m7 ____ T
2 ____ M7 ____ m7 ____ M2 ____ m2 ____ M7 ____ m7 ____ T ____ M2
3 ____ M2 ____ m2 ____ m2 ____ M2 ____ M7 ____ m7 ____ T ____ M7
4 ____ m7 ____ M2 ____ M7 ____ m2 ____ m2 ____ M7 ____ M2 ____ m7
5 ____ m7 ____ M2 ____ M7 ____ m2 ____ M7 ____ m2 ____ M2 ____ m7
6 ____ T ____ m7 ____ m7 ____ M2 ____ M2 ____ m7 ____ M7 ____ m2
7 ____ M7 ____ m2 ____ m2 ____ M7 ____ T ____ m7 ____ T ____ M7
8 ____ m7 ____ M2 ____ M7 ____ m2 ____ M7 ____ m2 ____ m7 ____ M2
9 ____ T ____ m7 ____ T ____ m7 ____ M7 ____ m2 ____ M2 ____ m7
10 ____ T ____ m7 ____ M7 ____ m2 ____ M2 ____ M7 ____ M7 ____ m7
11 ____ T ____ M7 ____ m7 ____ M7 ____ m2 ____ T ____ m7 ____ M7
12 ____ m2 ____ m7 ____ T ____ m7 ____ m7 ____ M7 ____ m2 ____ M7

A7-7 (COPY 3) Harmonic interval identification: major and minor seconds, tritones, major and minor sevenths

1 ____ m2 ____ M2 ____ m7 ____ M7 ____ T ____ m2 ____ m7 ____ T

2 ____ M7 ____ m7 ____ M2 ____ m2 ____ M7 ____ m7 ____ T ____ M2

3 ____ M2 ____ m2 ____ m2 ____ M2 ____ M7 ____ m7 ____ T ____ M7

4 ____ m7 ____ M2 ____ M7 ____ m2 ____ m2 ____ M7 ____ M2 ____ m7

5 ____ m7 ____ M2 ____ M7 ____ m2 ____ M7 ____ m2 ____ M2 ____ m7

6 ____ T ____ m7 ____ m7 ____ M2 ____ M2 ____ m7 ____ M7 ____ m2

7 ____ M7 ____ m2 ____ m2 ____ M7 ____ T ____ m7 ____ T ____ M7

8 ____ m7 ____ M2 ____ M7 ____ m2 ____ M7 ____ m2 ____ m7 ____ M2

9 ____ T ____ m7 ____ T ____ m7 ____ M7 ____ m2 ____ M2 ____ m7

10 ____ T ____ m7 ____ M7 ____ m2 ____ M2 ____ M7 ____ M7 ____ m7

11 ____ T ____ M7 ____ m7 ____ M7 ____ m2 ____ T ____ m7 ____ M7

12 ____ m2 ____ m7 ____ T ____ m7 ____ m7 ____ M7 ____ m2 ____ M7

A7-7 (COPY 4) Harmonic interval identification: major and minor seconds, tritones, major and minor sevenths

1 ____ m2 ____ M2 ____ m7 ____ M7 ____ T ____ m2 ____ m7 ____ T

2 ____ M7 ____ m7 ____ M2 ____ m2 ____ M7 ____ m7 ____ T ____ M2

3 ____ M2 ____ m2 ____ m2 ____ M2 ____ M7 ____ m7 ____ T ____ M7

4 ____ m7 ____ M2 ____ M7 ____ m2 ____ m2 ____ M7 ____ M2 ____ m7

5 ____ m7 ____ M2 ____ M7 ____ m2 ____ M7 ____ m2 ____ M2 ____ m7

6 ____ T ____ m7 ____ m7 ____ M2 ____ M2 ____ m7 ____ M7 ____ m2

7 ____ M7 ____ m2 ____ m2 ____ M7 ____ T ____ m7 ____ T ____ M7

8 ____ m7 ____ M2 ____ M7 ____ m2 ____ M7 ____ m2 ____ m7 ____ M2

9 ____ T ____ m7 ____ T ____ m7 ____ M7 ____ m2 ____ M2 ____ m7

10 ____ T ____ m7 ____ M7 ____ m2 ____ M2 ____ M7 ____ M7 ____ m7

11 ____ T ____ M7 ____ m7 ____ M7 ____ m2 ____ T ____ m7 ____ M7

12 ____ m2 ____ m7 ____ T ____ m7 ____ m7 ____ M7 ____ m2 ____ M7

A7-8 Harmonic interval identification: all intervals previously studied
(COPY 1)

1	____ M3	____ P4	____ M2	____ P5	____ M6	____ m7	____ M7	____ P8
2	____ M3	____ m3	____ M2	____ P5	____ P8	____ M7	____ M6	____ P5
3	____ M2	____ m3	____ M3	____ P4	____ m2	____ M2	____ m3	____ M3
4	____ M3	____ P4	____ T	____ P5	____ M6	____ m6	____ M7	____ P8
5	____ M6	____ m6	____ P5	____ P4	____ P4	____ M3	____ M2	____ m2
6	____ P8	____ M7	____ m7	____ M6	____ P5	____ M3	____ m6	____ m3
7	____ M3	____ m3	____ P5	____ M7	____ P5	____ M3	____ m3	____ m7
8	____ m3	____ P5	____ M3	____ m7	____ M6	____ P4	____ M2	____ P5
9	____ P5	____ m3	____ M3	____ m6	____ m7	____ P8	____ P4	____ M2
10	____ P8	____ m7	____ M3	____ P5	____ m3	____ M3	____ M6	____ P8
11	____ m6	____ P5	____ m2	____ M3	____ M6	____ m6	____ M3	____ m3
12	____ m2	____ M6	____ T	____ M6	____ P5	____ T	____ M6	____ M3

A7-8 Harmonic interval identification: all intervals previously studied
(COPY 2)

1	____ M3	____ P4	____ M2	____ P5	____ M6	____ m7	____ M7	____ P8
2	____ M3	____ m3	____ M2	____ P5	____ P8	____ M7	____ M6	____ P5
3	____ M2	____ m3	____ M3	____ P4	____ m2	____ M2	____ m3	____ M3
4	____ M3	____ P4	____ T	____ P5	____ M6	____ m6	____ M7	____ P8
5	____ M6	____ m6	____ P5	____ P4	____ P4	____ M3	____ M2	____ m2
6	____ P8	____ M7	____ m7	____ M6	____ P5	____ M3	____ m6	____ m3
7	____ M3	____ m3	____ P5	____ M7	____ P5	____ M3	____ m3	____ m7
8	____ m3	____ P5	____ M3	____ m7	____ M6	____ P4	____ M2	____ P5
9	____ P5	____ m3	____ M3	____ m6	____ m7	____ P8	____ P4	____ M2
10	____ P8	____ m7	____ M3	____ P5	____ m3	____ M3	____ M6	____ P8
11	____ m6	____ P5	____ m2	____ M3	____ M6	____ m6	____ M3	____ m3
12	____ m2	____ M6	____ T	____ M6	____ P5	____ T	____ M6	____ M3

A7-8 Harmonic interval identification: all intervals previously studied
(COPY 3)

1	____ M3	____ P4	____ M2	____ P5	____ M6	____ m7	____ M7	____ P8
2	____ M3	____ m3	____ M2	____ P5	____ P8	____ M7	____ M6	____ P5
3	____ M2	____ m3	____ M3	____ P4	____ m2	____ M2	____ m3	____ M3
4	____ M3	____ P4	____ T	____ P5	____ M6	____ m6	____ M7	____ P8
5	____ M6	____ m6	____ P5	____ P4	____ P4	____ M3	____ M2	____ m2
6	____ P8	____ M7	____ m7	____ M6	____ P5	____ M3	____ m6	____ m3
7	____ M3	____ m3	____ P5	____ M7	____ P5	____ M3	____ m3	____ m7
8	____ m3	____ P5	____ M3	____ m7	____ M6	____ P4	____ M2	____ P5
9	____ P5	____ m3	____ M3	____ m6	____ m7	____ P8	____ P4	____ M2
10	____ P8	____ m7	____ M3	____ P5	____ m3	____ M3	____ M6	____ P8
11	____ m6	____ P5	____ m2	____ M3	____ M6	____ m6	____ M3	____ m3
12	____ m2	____ M6	____ T	____ M6	____ P5	____ T	____ M6	____ M3

A7-8 Harmonic interval identification: all intervals previously studied
(COPY 4)

1	____ M3	____ P4	____ M2	____ P5	____ M6	____ m7	____ M7	____ P8
2	____ M3	____ m3	____ M2	____ P5	____ P8	____ M7	____ M6	____ P5
3	____ M2	____ m3	____ M3	____ P4	____ m2	____ M2	____ m3	____ M3
4	____ M3	____ P4	____ T	____ P5	____ M6	____ m6	____ M7	____ P8
5	____ M6	____ m6	____ P5	____ P4	____ P4	____ M3	____ M2	____ m2
6	____ P8	____ M7	____ m7	____ M6	____ P5	____ M3	____ m6	____ m3
7	____ M3	____ m3	____ P5	____ M7	____ P5	____ M3	____ m3	____ m7
8	____ m3	____ P5	____ M3	____ m7	____ M6	____ P4	____ M2	____ P5
9	____ P5	____ m3	____ M3	____ m6	____ m7	____ P8	____ P4	____ M2
10	____ P8	____ m7	____ M3	____ P5	____ m3	____ M3	____ M6	____ P8
11	____ m6	____ P5	____ m2	____ M3	____ M6	____ m6	____ M3	____ m3
12	____ m2	____ M6	____ T	____ M6	____ P5	____ T	____ M6	____ M3

PART B

MELODY AND RHYTHM

INTRODUCTION

Part B contains 17 series designed to develop skills in sightsinging and melodic dictation. In a few series, the student responds only to rhythm; in some others, rhythmic aspects are minimalized to permit emphasis on melodic and notational problems. Most of the series, however, deal with both rhythmic and melodic problems.

The musical material begins with short rhythmic and melodic segments, and progresses to complete melodies, some with modulations. A wide range of difficulty is represented, beginning with very simple patterns and gradually advancing to complex rhythmic and melodic problems.

The series in Part B can be studied in the order in which they appear. Or where desired, either the sightsinging series or the dictation series can be worked through independently of the other. Another possibility is to begin sightsinging and dictation at the same time, and to practice these two skills together where they deal with similar musical content. A recommended syllabus to accomplish this is given below. In it the series are grouped into six study units, each dealing with rather similar problems and levels of difficulty. Within the study units (with some exceptions noted), series can be begun together or in any order. The units, on the other hand, should be done in order.

SYLLABUS FOR THE CONCURRENT STUDY OF SIGHTSINGING AND DICTATION

Unit 1

Series B1 Elementary rhythmic dictation
Series B2 Elementary sightsinging
Series B3 Elementary melodic dictation

Unit 2

Series B4 Intermediate rhythmic dictation
Series B5 Intermediate sightsinging
Series B6 Intermediate melodic dictation

Unit 3

Series B7 Sightsinging: complete phrases
Series B8 Rhythmic dictation: bar lines and meter
Series B9 Melodic dictation: complete phrases

Unit 4

Series B10 Sightsinging: skips and accidentals
Series B11 Melodic dictation: skips and accidentals

Unit 5

Series B12 Sightsinging: modulations
Series B13 Advanced sightsinging
Series B14 Advanced melodic dictation

Unit 6

Series B15	Sightsinging: complete phrases with modulations
Series B16	Rhythmic dictation: complete phrases with modulations
Series B17	Sightsinging: complete phrases

In Unit 3, B8 should precede B9. In Unit 5, B12 should precede B13. In Unit 6, B15 should precede B16. In all other cases, series in the same unit may be studied concurrently.

SUPPLEMENTAL CLASS MATERIALS

In addition to the individualized programmed materials that form the main body of these series, there are supplemental melodies intended primarily for class use. These serve a number of purposes: 1) Idioms found in the lessons can be incorporated into longer phrases. 2) The type of material found in the lessons can be concurrent with class activity. 3) The student can get feedback from the teacher. 4) The teacher can observe student responses. 5) The teacher can give input to help the student correct and refine responses.

The supplemental sightsinging melodies are found at the end of each series. The dictation melodies are placed in the Instructor's Manual.

One of the principal purposes of this book is to develop the student's ability to sing melodies from printed music at first sight. First-sight performance is implied in the term sightsinging, but sometimes the term is used to include the singing of practiced materials, which might be called "prepared sightsinging." All the materials of the programmed lessons in this book are intended for the development of reading at first sight. The supplemental materials for each lesson, however, are arranged to be used either way.

SERIES B1

ELEMENTARY RHYTHMIC DICTATION

The purpose of this series is to develop the ability to write the rhythm of melodies you hear. While the melodies of this series contain both pitches and rhythms, here you should write only the rhythm. A printed worksheet and a tape recording are provided for each lesson.

The lessons are made up of short rhythmic patterns. For each pattern on the worksheet, there is a space in which you will write. To the right of this is a notation of the rhythm you will hear. To do a lesson, use a shield to cover the printed answer on the first pattern, then start the tape. When you have heard the first rhythmic pattern, stop the tape and write the notes for the rhythm you have heard. Slide the shield to the right to check your answer. Then start the tape and go on to the next pattern.

BI-I Rhythmic dictation

(COPY 1)

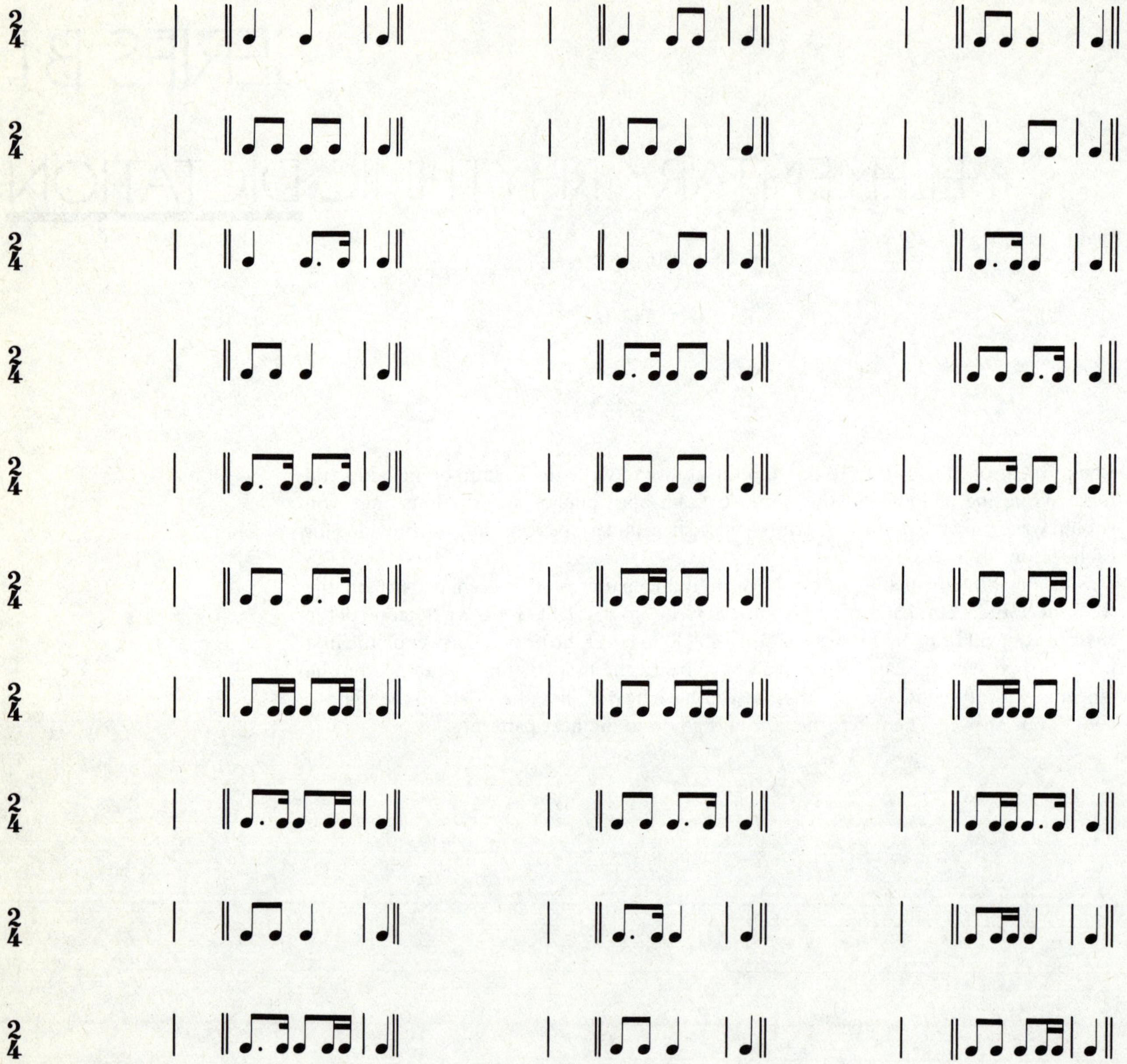

2/4

2/4

2/4

2/4

2/4

2/4

2/4

2/4

2/4

2/4

2/4

2/4

2/4

2/4

2/4

2/4

2/4

2/4

2/4

2/4

BI-I Rhythmic dictation

(COPY 2)

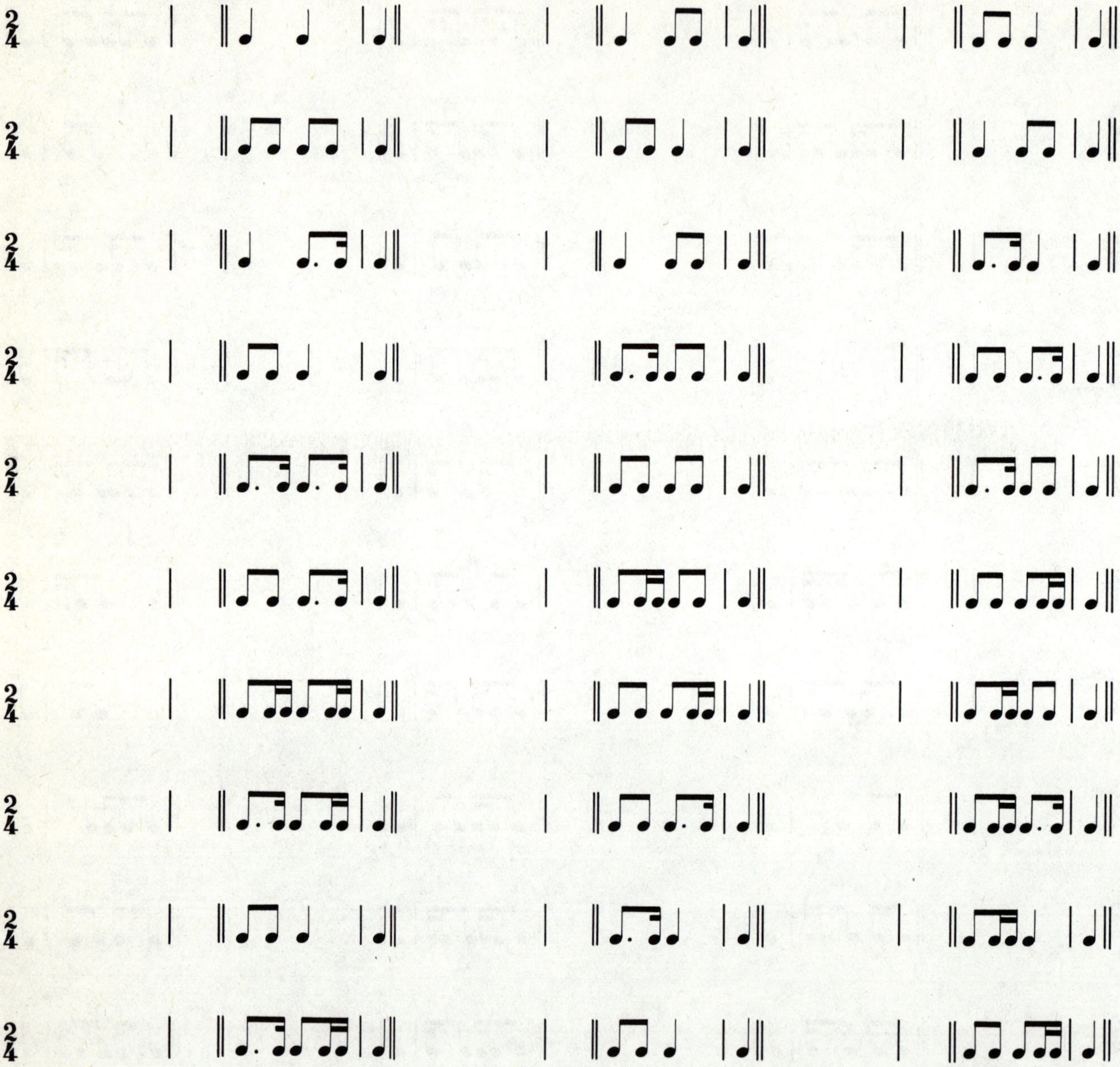

2/4

2/4

2/4

2/4

2/4

2/4

2/4

2/4

2/4

2/4

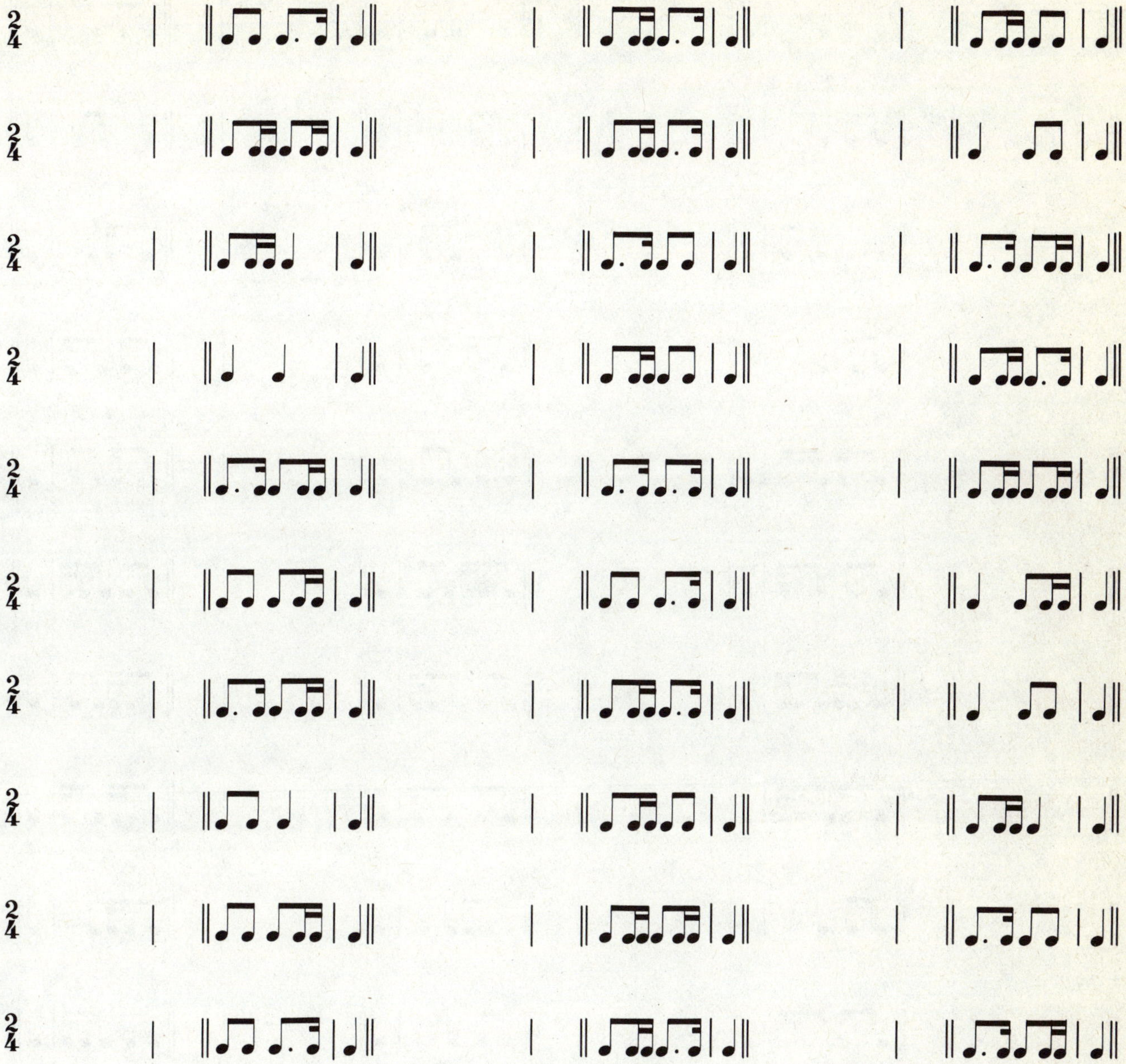

2/4

2/4

2/4

2/4

2/4

2/4

2/4

2/4

2/4

2/4

B1-1 Rhythmic dictation
(COPY 3)

2/4

2/4

2/4

2/4

2/4

2/4

2/4

2/4

2/4

2/4

2/4

2/4

2/4

2/4

2/4

2/4

2/4

2/4

2/4

2/4

BI-2 Rhythmic dictation
(COPY I)

2/4

2/4

2/4

2/4

2/4

2/4

2/4

2/4

2/4

2/4

2/4

2/4

2/4

2/4

2/4

2/4

2/4

2/4

2/4

2/4

B1-2 Rhythmic dictation
(COPY 2)

2/4

2/4

2/4

2/4

2/4

2/4

2/4

2/4

2/4

2/4

B1-2 Rhythmic dictation
(COPY 3)

2/4

2/4

2/4

2/4

2/4

2/4

2/4

2/4

2/4

2/4

BI-3 Rhythmic dictation
(COPY 1)

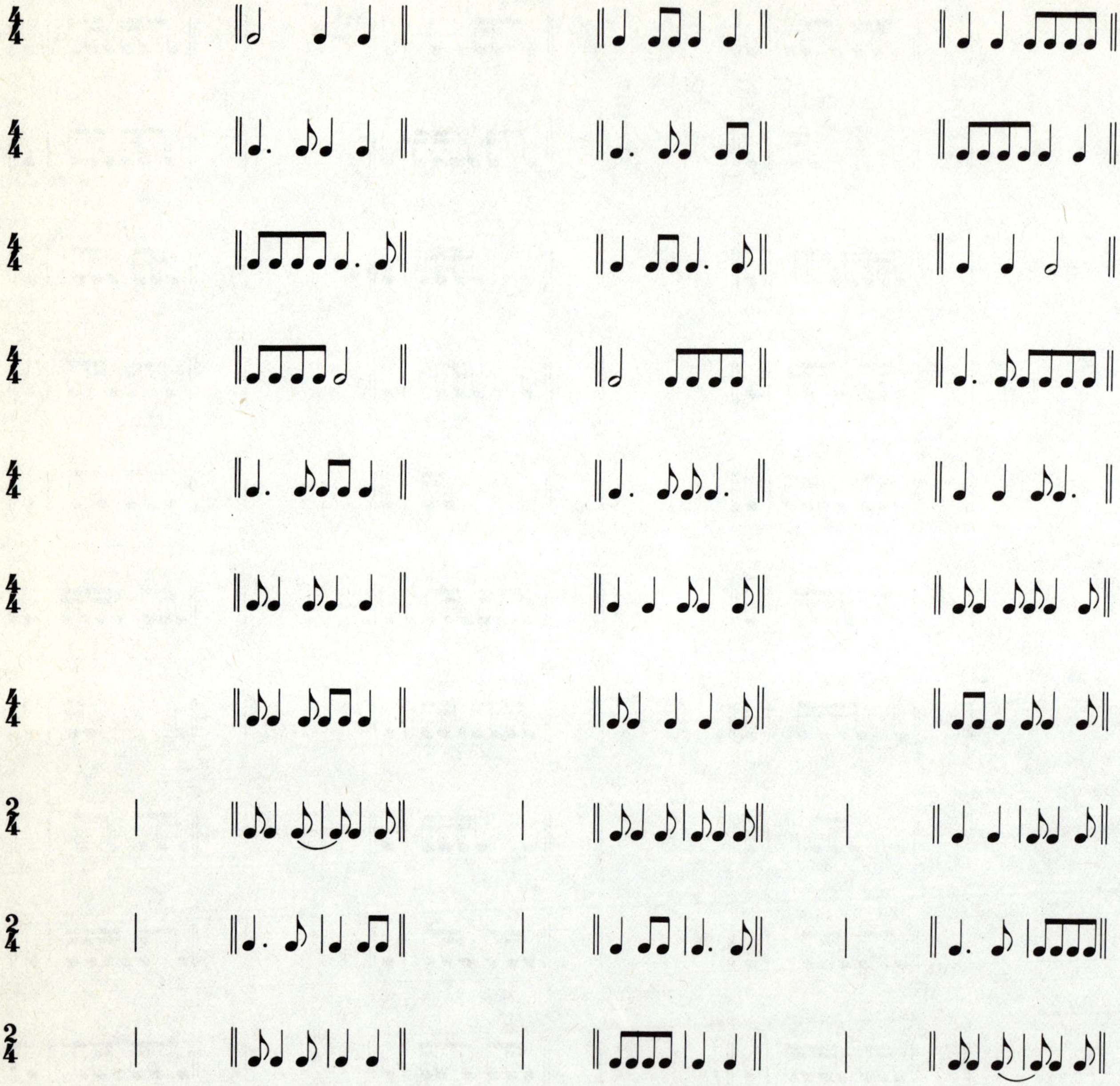

4/4

4/4

4/4

4/4

2/4

4/4

4/4

4/4

2/4

4/4

B1-3 Rhythmic dictation
(COPY 2)

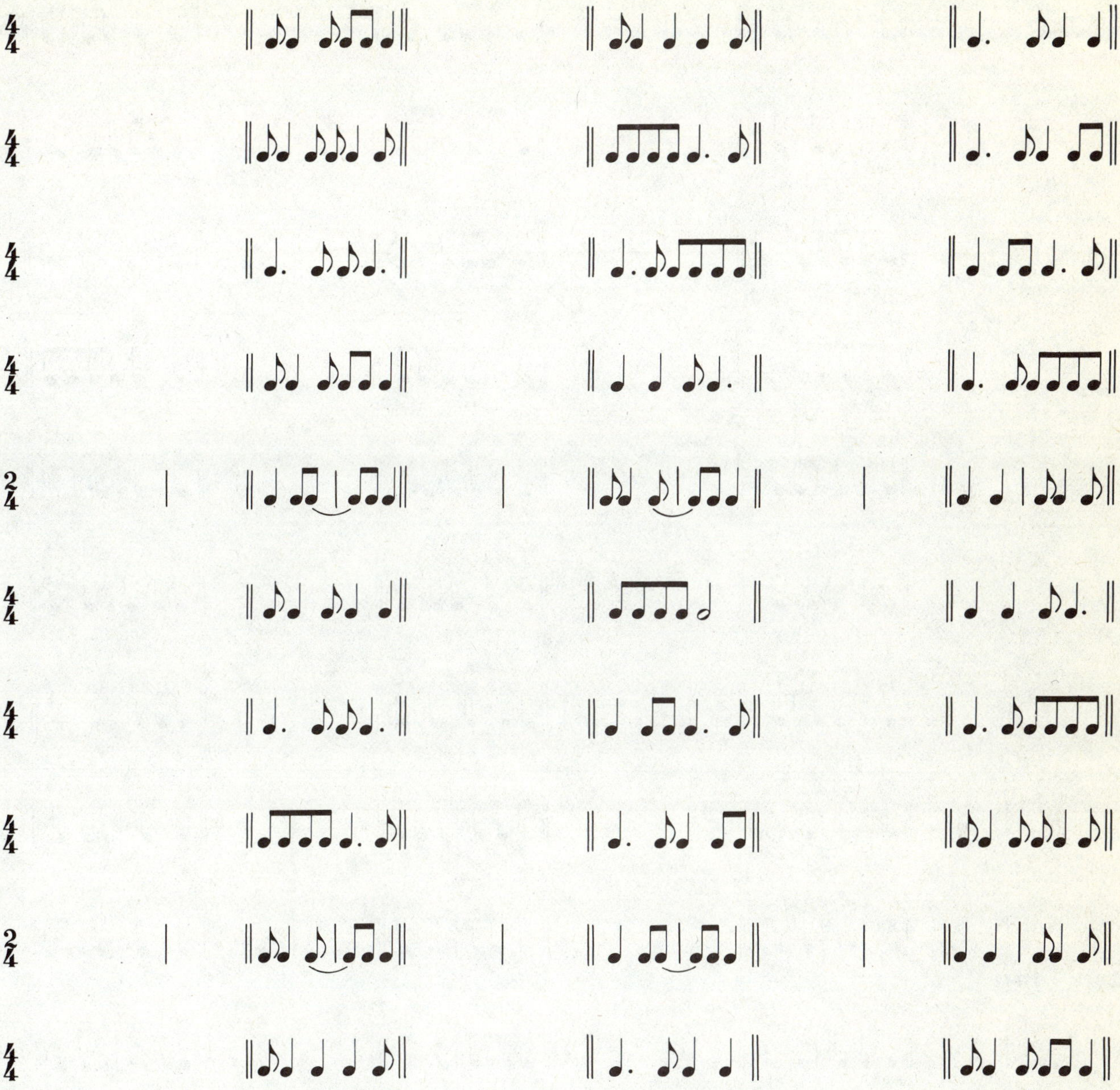

4/4

4/4

4/4

4/4

2/4

4/4

4/4

4/4

2/4

4/4

B1-3 Rhythmic dictation
(COPY 3)

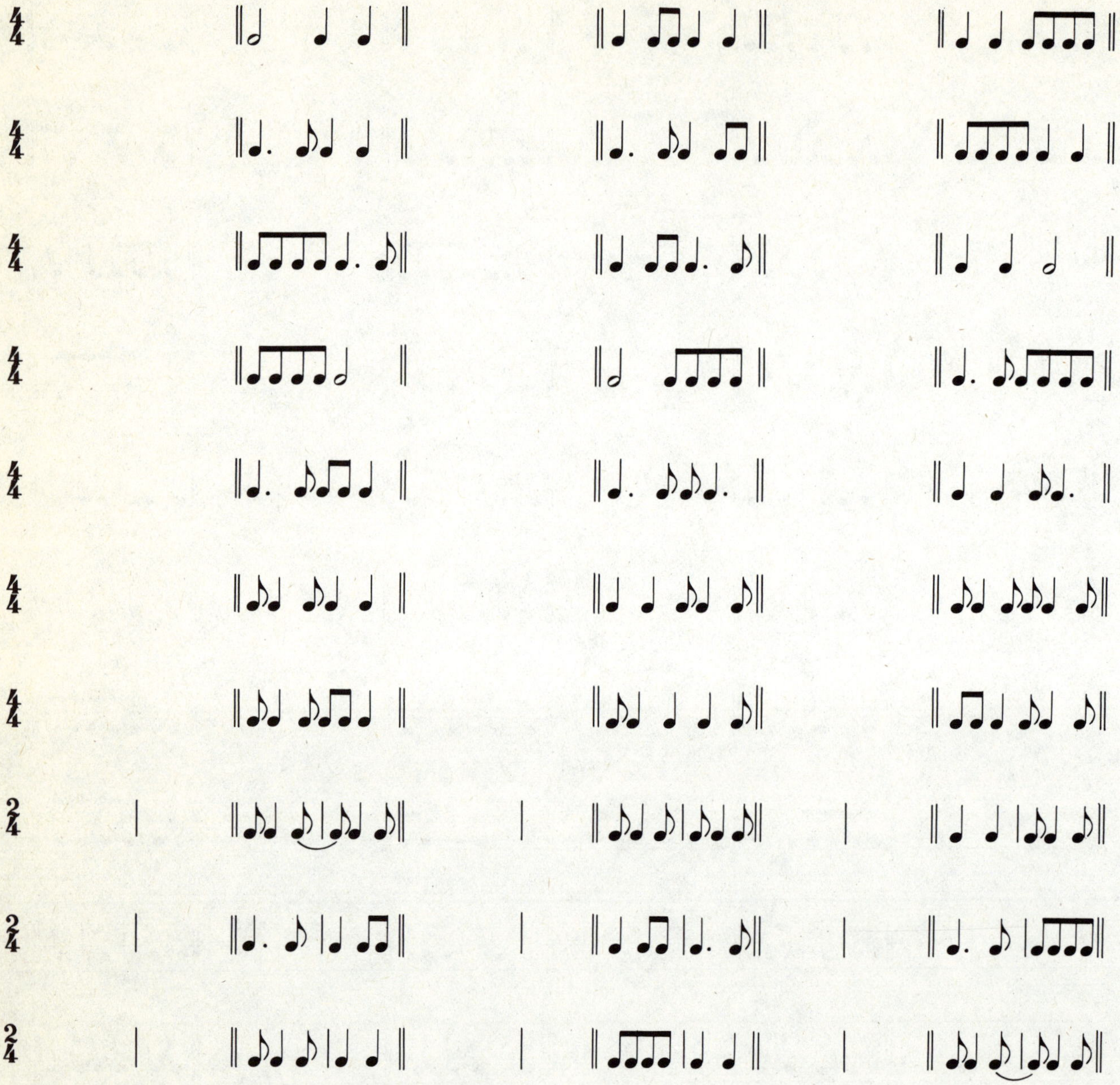

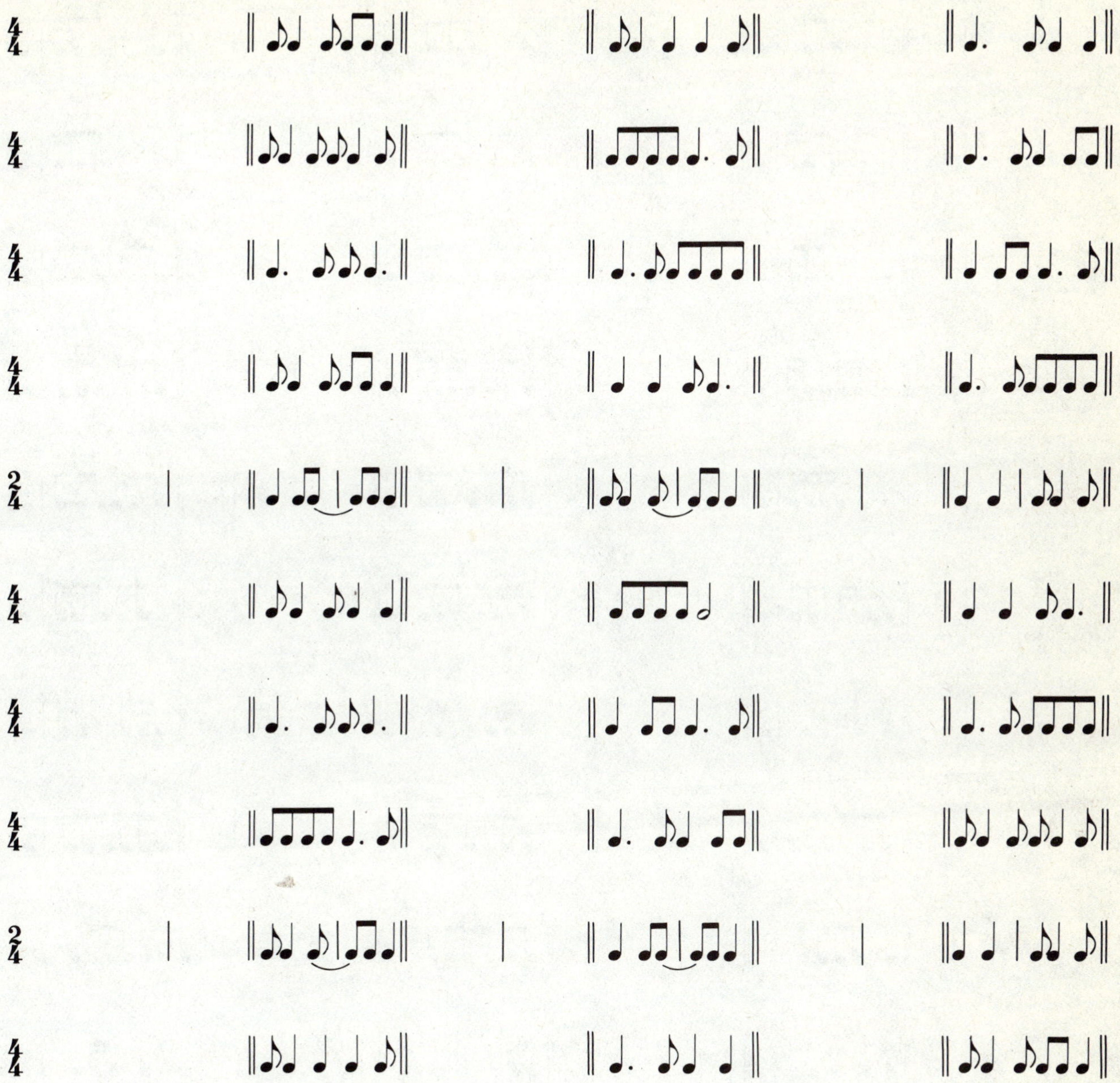

BI-4 Rhythmic dictation

(COPY 1)

2/4

2/4

2/4

2/4

2/4

2/4

2/4

2/4

4/4

4/4

4/4

2/4

2/4

2/4

2/4

2/4

2/4

2/4

2/4

2/4

B1-4 Rhythmic dictation
(COPY 2)

4/4

2/4

2/4

2/4

2/4

2/4

2/4

2/4

2/4

2/4

B1-4 Rhythmic dictation
(COPY 3)

4/4

2/4

2/4

2/4

2/4

2/4

2/4

2/4

2/4

2/4

SERIES B2

ELEMENTARY SIGHTSINGING

The purpose of the sightsinging lessons is to develop the ability to sing melodies from the printed page at sight. A printed score and a tape recording are provided for each lesson.

The lessons are made up of short melodies. To do a lesson, start the tape and you will hear a metronome giving the tempo and the first pitch of the first melody. You immediately should sing the written melody with the metronome. You will then hear the melody performed correctly. Move on, singing the next melody, and again listen to the melody on the tape. You will be given the starting tone only for the first melody. The starting tone for each of the others can be judged from the pitches of the preceding melody.

It is important to be critical as you compare your performance with that on the tape. Be sure that both the pitches and the rhythms are correct.

Depending on the range of your voice, you may find it necessary to sing in an octave different from that on the tape, and you may find that you must change octaves in the course of a lesson. Sing in the most comfortable register at all times.

B2-1 Sightsinging

B2-2 Sightsinging

B2-3 Sightsinging

B2-4 Sightsinging

B2-5 Sightsinging

B2-6 Sightsinging

B2-7 Sightsinging

B2-1 Lesson supplements

B2-2 Lesson supplements

B2-3 Lesson supplements

B2-4 Lesson supplements

B2-5 Lesson supplements

B2-6 Lesson supplements

B2-7 Lesson supplements

SERIES B3

ELEMENTARY MELODIC DICTATION

The purpose of this series is to develop the ability to write both the pitch and the rhythm of melodies you hear. A printed worksheet and a tape recording are provided for each lesson.

These lessons are made up of short melodies. For each melody on the worksheet, there is a space in which you will write. To the right of this is a notation of the correct answer. To do a lesson, use a shield to cover the printed answer on the first melody, and start the tape. When you have heard the first melody, stop the tape and write the notes of the melody you heard. You should write both the pitches and the rhythm. Then slide the shield to the right to check your answer. Start the tape and go on to the next melody.

B3-1 **Melodic dictation**
(COPY 1)

B3-1 Melodic dictation
(COPY 2)

B3-1 Melodic dictation
(COPY 3)

B3-2 Melodic dictation

(COPY 1)

B3-2 Melodic dictation
(COPY 2)

B3-2 Melodic dictation

(COPY 3)

B3-3 Melodic dictation
(COPY 1)

B3-3 Melodic dictation

(COPY 2)

B3-3 Melodic dictation
(COPY 3)

B3-4 Melodic dictation

(COPY 1)

B3-4 Melodic dictation

(COPY 2)

B3-4 Melodic dictation
(COPY 3)

SERIES B4

INTERMEDIATE RHYTHMIC DICTATION

The purpose and the procedure for this series are the same as for Series B1, which should be done first. A worksheet and a tape recording are provided for each lesson.

The lessons are made up of short rhythmic patterns. For each pattern on the worksheet, there is a space in which you will write. To the right of this is a notation of the rhythm you will hear. To do a lesson, use a shield to cover the printed answer on the first pattern, and start the tape. When you have heard the first rhythmic pattern, stop the tape and write the notes for the rhythm you have heard. Slide the shield to the right to check your answer. Then start the tape and go on to the next pattern.

B4-1 Rhythmic dictation

(COPY 1)

$\frac{3}{4}$

$\frac{3}{4}$

$\frac{3}{4}$

$\frac{3}{4}$

$\frac{3}{4}$

$\frac{3}{4}$

$\frac{3}{4}$

$\frac{3}{4}$

$\frac{3}{4}$

$\frac{3}{4}$

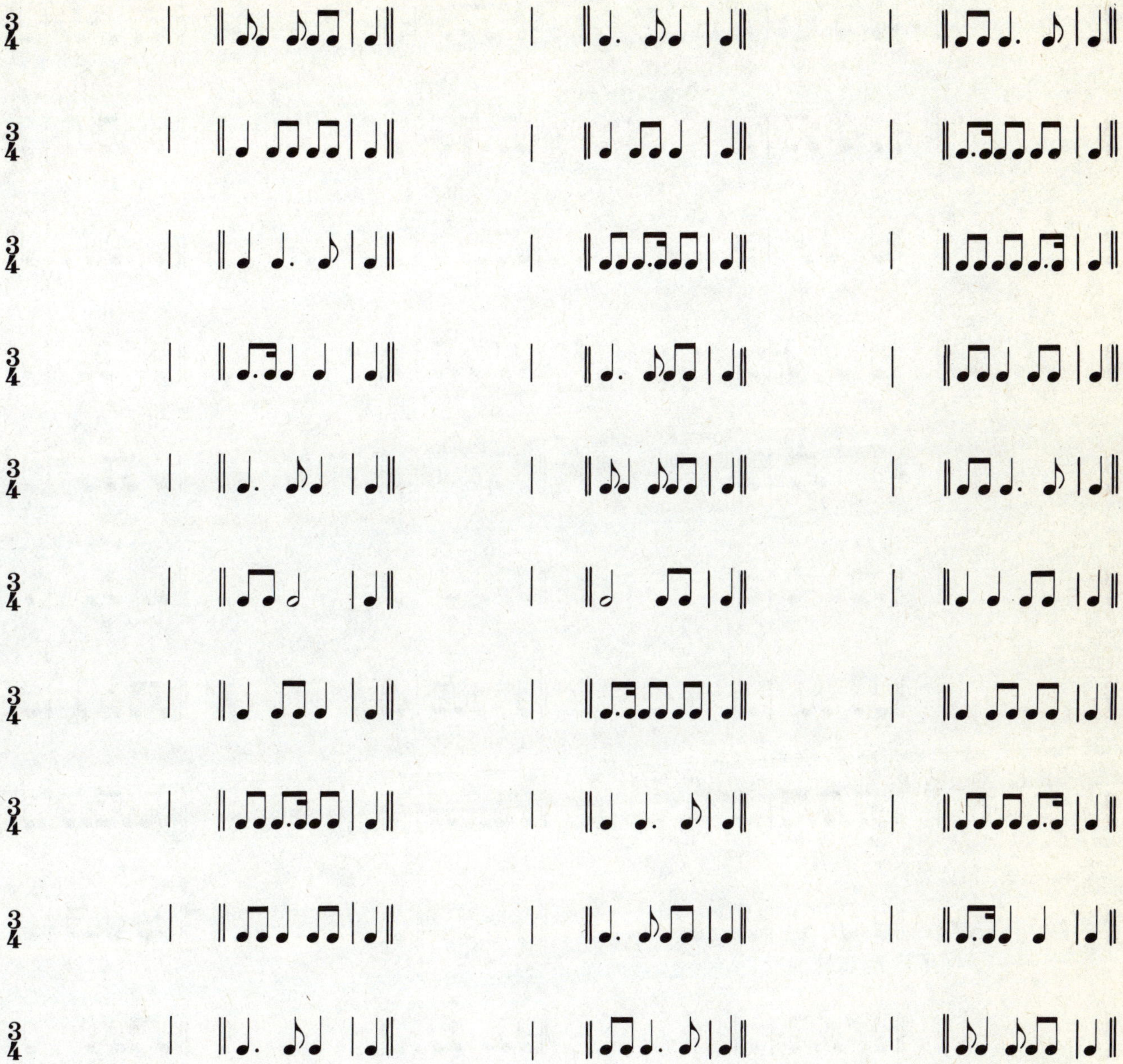

3/4

3/4

3/4

3/4

3/4

3/4

3/4

3/4

3/4

3/4

B4-1 Rhythmic dictation
(COPY 2)

3/4

3/4

3/4

3/4

3/4

3/4

3/4

3/4

3/4

3/4

3/4

3/4

3/4

3/4

3/4

3/4

3/4

3/4

3/4

3/4

B4-1 Rhythmic dictation
(COPY 3)

$\frac{3}{4}$

$\frac{3}{4}$

$\frac{3}{4}$

$\frac{3}{4}$

$\frac{3}{4}$

$\frac{3}{4}$

$\frac{3}{4}$

$\frac{3}{4}$

$\frac{3}{4}$

$\frac{3}{4}$

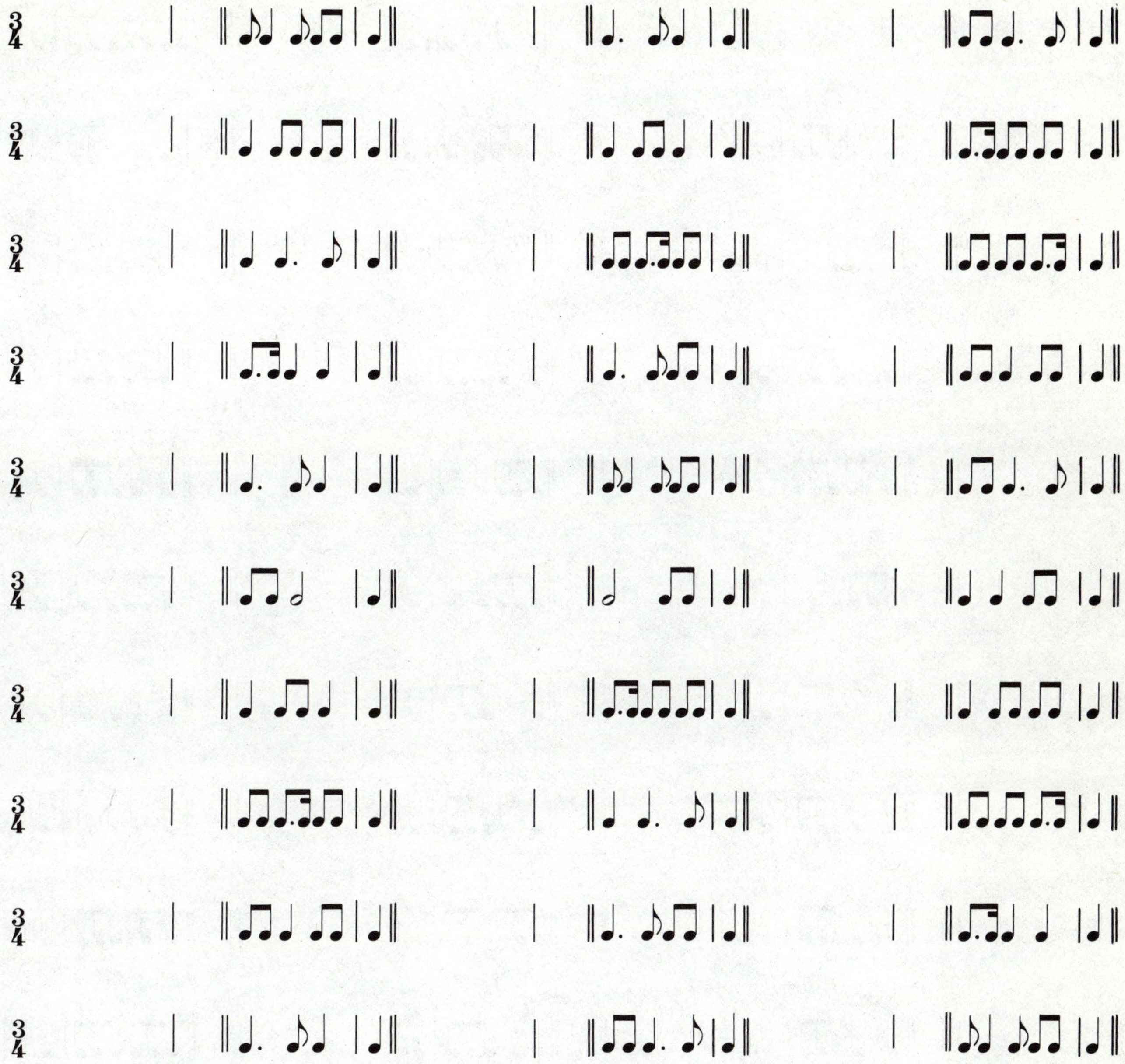

3
4

3
4

3
4

3
4

3
4

3
4

3
4

3
4

3
4

3
4

B4-2 Rhythmic dictation

(COPY 1)

6
8

6
8

6
8

6
8

6
8

6
8

6
8

6
8

6
8

6
8

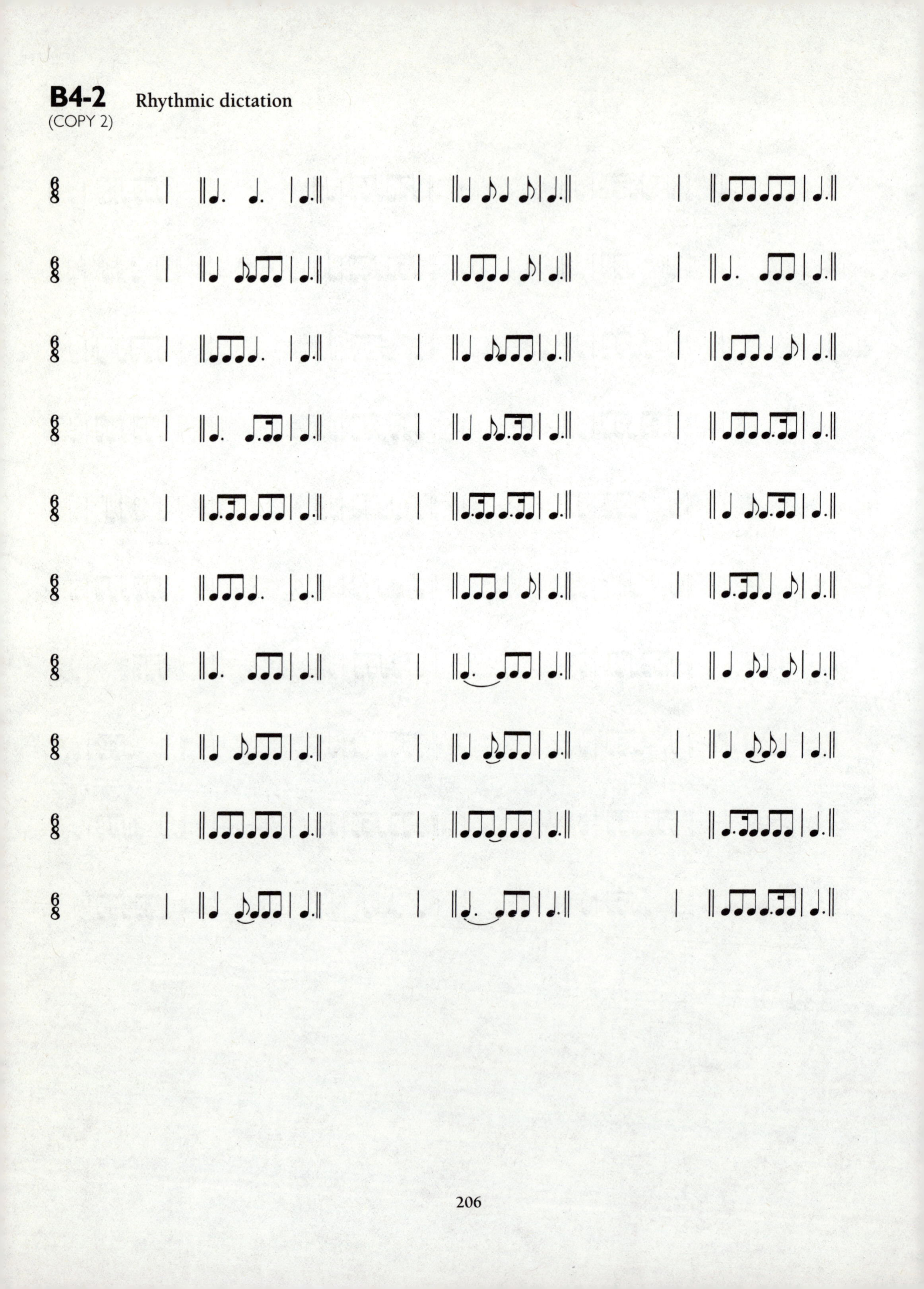

B4-2 Rhythmic dictation
(COPY 2)

$\frac{6}{8}$

$\frac{6}{8}$

$\frac{6}{8}$

$\frac{6}{8}$

$\frac{6}{8}$

$\frac{6}{8}$

$\frac{6}{8}$

$\frac{6}{8}$

$\frac{6}{8}$

$\frac{6}{8}$

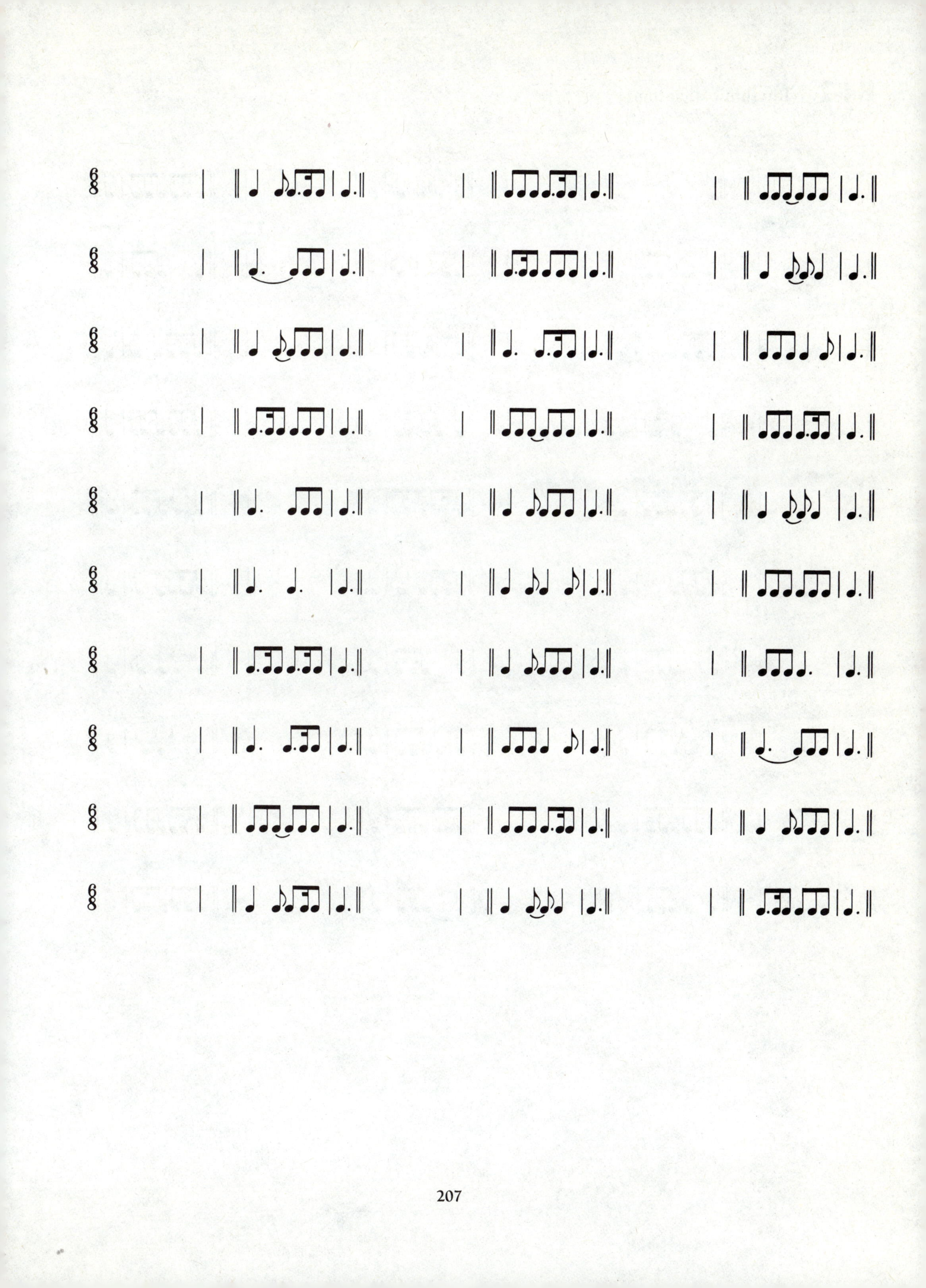

6/8

6/8

6/8

6/8

6/8

6/8

6/8

6/8

6/8

6/8

B4-2 Rhythmic dictation
(COPY 3)

6
8

6
8

6
8

6
8

6
8

6
8

6
8

6
8

6
8

6
8

B4-3 Rhythmic dictation
(COPY 1)

♩. = 76

9/8

9/8

9/8

9/8

9/8

9/8

♪ = 180

6/8

6/8

6/8

6/8

♩. = 60

6/8

6/8

6/8

6/8

6/8

♩. = 76

9/8

9/8

♪ = 180

6/8

♩. = 60

6/8

6/8

B4-3 Rhythmic dictation
(COPY 2)

♩. = 60

6/8

6/8

6/8

6/8

6/8

♩. = 76

9/8

9/8

♪ = 180

6/8

♩. = 60

6/8

6/8

B4-3 Rhythmic dictation
(COPY 3)

♩. = 76

9/8

9/8

9/8

9/8

9/8

9/8

♪ = 180

6/8

6/8

6/8

6/8

♩. = 60

6/8

6/8

6/8

6/8

6/8

♩. = 76

9/8

9/8

♪ = 180

6/8

♩. = 60

6/8

6/8

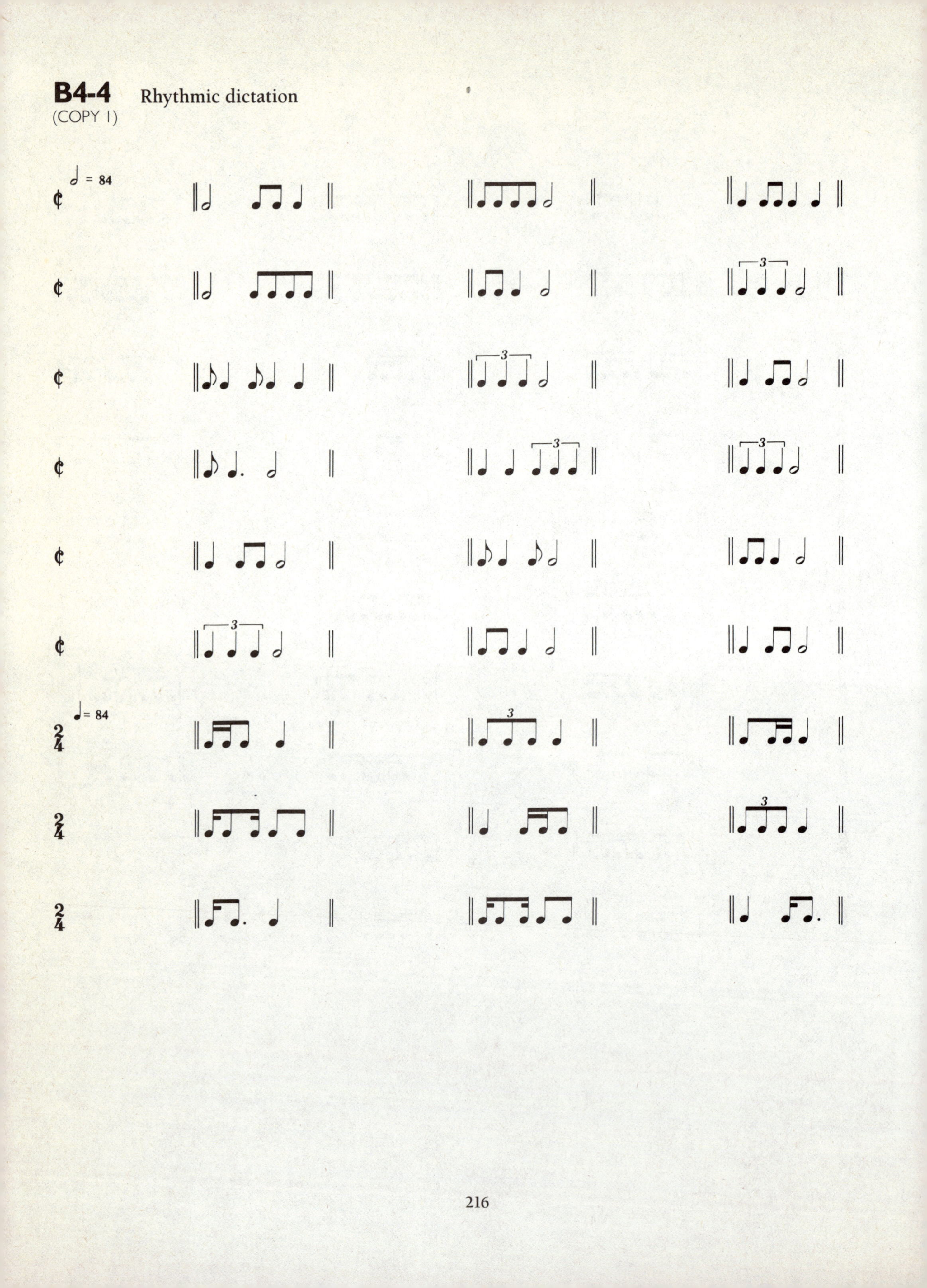

B4-4 Rhythmic dictation
(COPY 1)

= 84

= 84

♪ = 84

4/8

4/8

4/8

4/8

4/8

4/8

𝅗𝅥 = 84

¢

3

¢

3

♩ = 84

2/4

3

♪ = 84

4/8

4/8

B4-4 Rhythmic dictation
(COPY 2)

$𝅗𝅥$ = 84

¢

3 3 3 3 3

$♩$ = 84

2/4

3 3

♪ = 84

4/8

4/8

4/8

4/8

4/8

4/8

𝅗𝅥 = 84

¢ 3

¢ 3

♩ = 84

2/4 3

♪ = 84

4/8

4/8

B4-4 **Rhythmic dictation**
(COPY 3)

𝅗𝅥 = 84

¢

¢

¢

¢

¢

¢

♩= 84

2/4

2/4

2/4

♪ = 84

$\frac{4}{8}$

$\frac{4}{8}$

$\frac{4}{8}$

$\frac{4}{8}$

$\frac{4}{8}$

$\frac{4}{8}$

𝅗𝅥 = 84

¢ 3

¢ 3

♩ = 84

$\frac{2}{4}$ 3

♪ = 84

$\frac{4}{8}$

$\frac{4}{8}$

SERIES B5

INTERMEDIATE SIGHTSINGING

The purpose and the procedure for this series are the same as for Series B2, which should be done first. A printed score and a tape recording are provided for each lesson.

The lessons are made up of short melodies. To do a lesson, start the tape, and you will hear a metronome giving the tempo and the first pitch of the first melody. You immediately should sing the written melody with the metronome. You will then hear the melody performed correctly. Move on, singing the next melody, and again listen to the melody on the tape. You will be given the starting tone only for the first melody. The starting tone for each of the others can be judged from the pitches of the preceding melody.

B5-I Sightsinging

B5-2 Sightsinging

B5-3 Sightsinging

B5-4 Sightsinging

B5-5 Sightsinging

B5-6 Sightsinging

3
3
3
3
3

B5-7 Sightsinging

B5-8 Sightsinging

B5-1 Lesson supplements

B5-2 Lesson supplements

B5-3 Lesson supplements

B5-4 Lesson supplements

B5-5 Lesson supplements

B5-6 Lesson supplements

B5-7 Lesson supplements

1
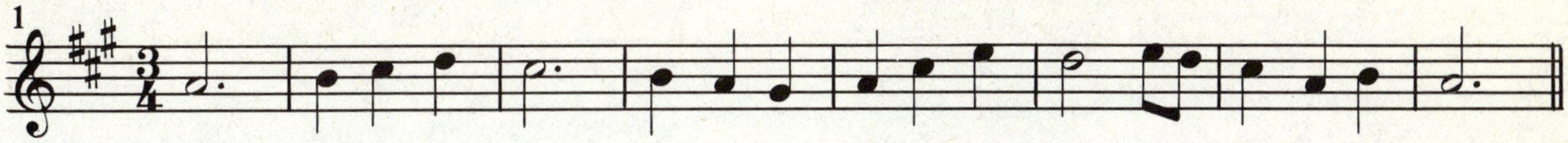

2
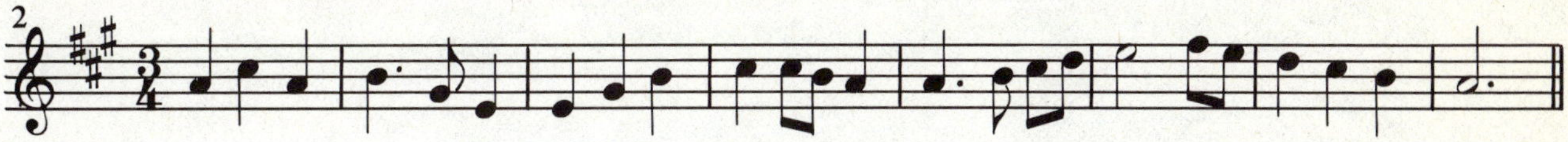

3
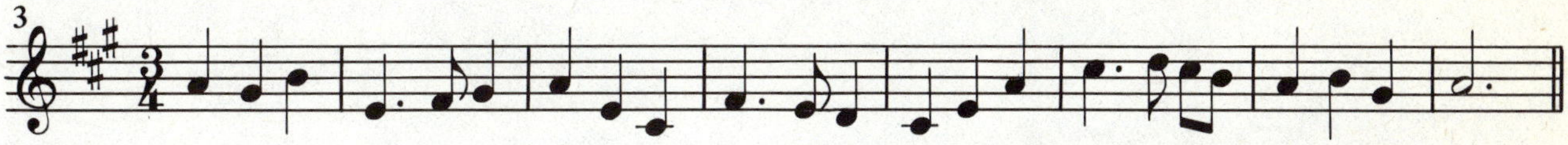

4
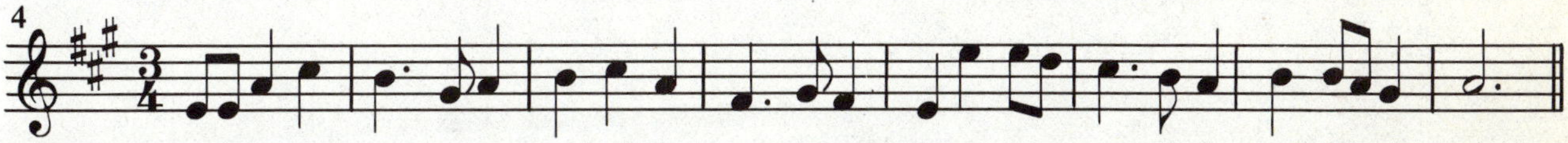

5
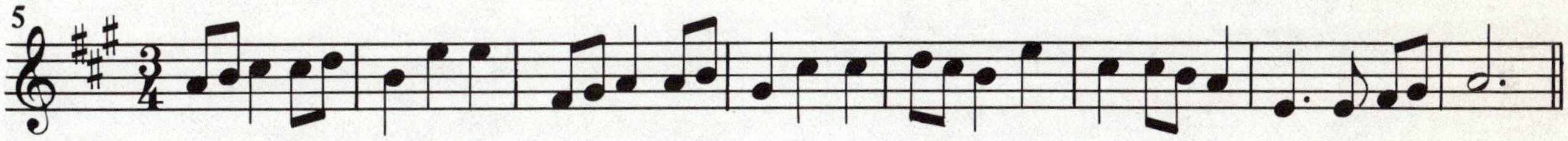

6
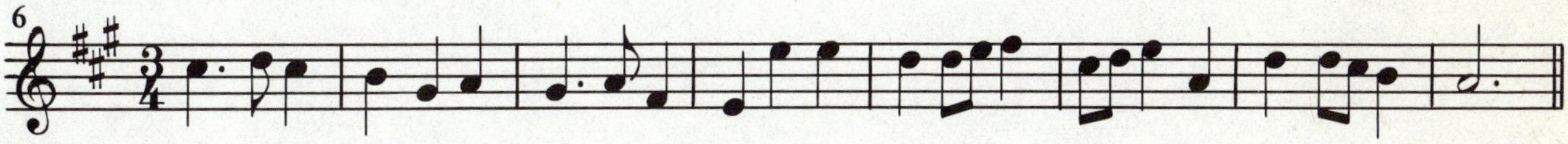

B5-8 Lesson supplements

1

2

3

4

5

6

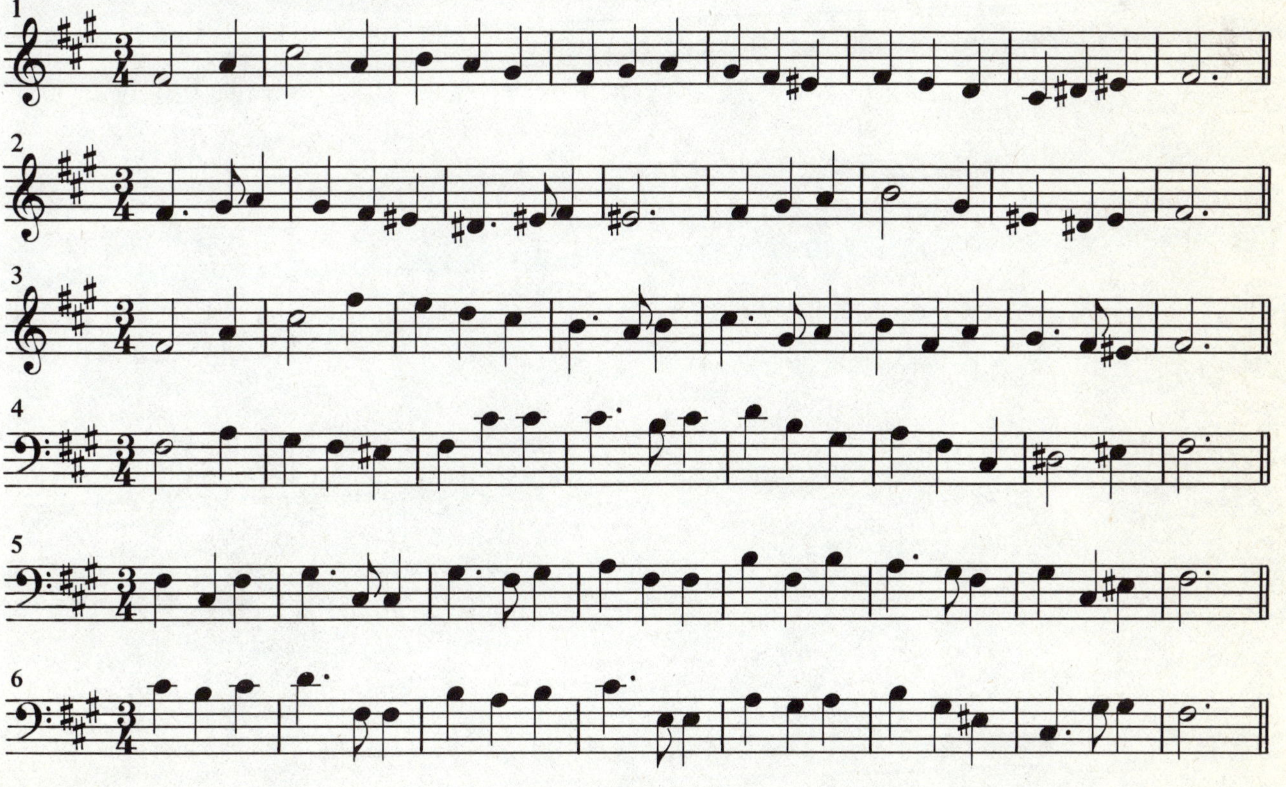

SERIES B6

INTERMEDIATE MELODIC DICTATION

The purpose of this series is to develop the ability to write both the pitch and the rhythm of melodies you hear. A printed worksheet and a tape recording are provided for each lesson.

The procedure is the same as for Series B3. The lessons are made up of short melodies. For each melody on the worksheet, there is a space in which you will write. To the right of this is a notation of the correct answer. To do a lesson, use a shield to cover the printed answer on the first melody, and start the tape. When you have heard the first melody, stop the tape and write the notes of the melody you heard. You should write both the pitches and the rhythm. Then slide the shield to the right to check your answer. Start the tape and go on to the next melody.

B6-1 Melodic dictation

(COPY 1)

B6-1 Melodic dictation
(COPY 2)

B6-1 Melodic dictation
(COPY 3)

B6-2 Melodic dictation
(COPY 1)

3
3
3
3
3
3
3
3
3
3
3
3
3
3
3
3
3
3
3

B6-2 Melodic dictation
(COPY 2)

B6-2 Melodic dictation
(COPY 3)

B6-3 Melodic dictation

(COPY 1)

B6-3 Melodic dictation
(COPY 2)

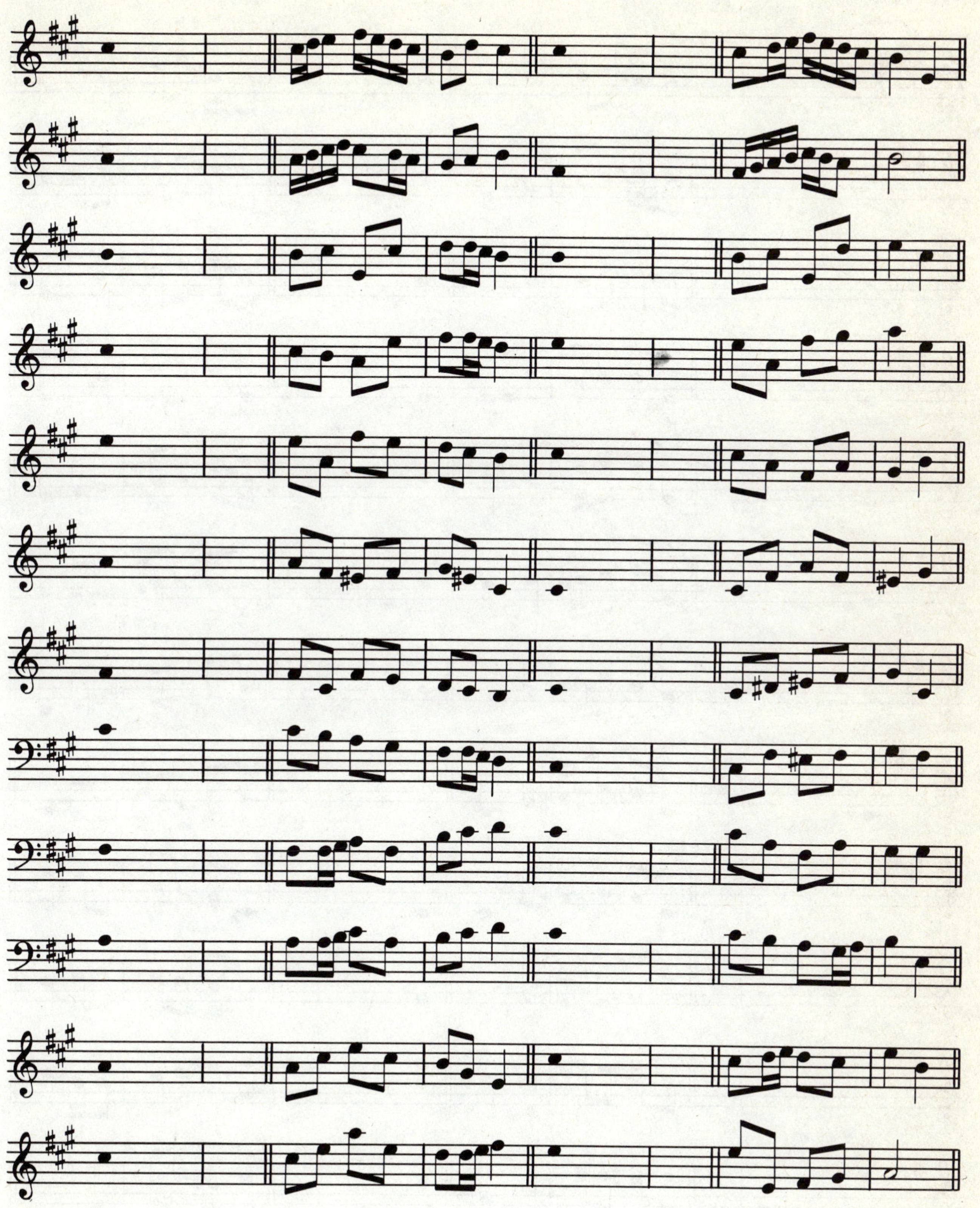

B6-3 Melodic dictation

(COPY 3)

B6-4 Melodic dictation

(COPY 1)

B6-4 Melodic dictation
(COPY 2)

B6-4 Melodic dictation

(COPY 3)

SERIES B7

SIGHTSINGING OF COMPLETE MELODIES

The purpose of this series is to develop the ability to sightsing complete melodies. A printed score and a tape recording are provided for each lesson.

Each melody fills an entire line. Before starting each melody, observe the metronome marking and the value of the note that will receive one beat. Observe the key signature to determine the key and the degree of the key on which the melody begins. For those melodies that do not begin on the tonic, it may be helpful to sing scalewise from the starting note to the tonic to help establish the key in your mind.

To do the lesson, start the tape recording. You will hear the metronome giving the tempo and the starting tone for the first melody. Stop the tape after hearing this, and sing the first melody. Start the tape again to hear the melody correctly performed, followed by the tempo and the starting tone for the next melody.

B7-I Sightsinging

11
♩. = 72
12
♩ = 144
13
♩ = 120
14
♩ = 116
15
♩ = 116
16
♪ = 144
17
♩ = 120
18
♩ = 112
19
♩. = 76
20
♩ = 116

B7-2 Sightsinging

11
♩= 100
12
♩= 132
13
♩= 104
14
♩= 100
15
♩.= 76
16
♩= 108
17
♩= 108
18
♩.= 84
19
♩= 88
20
♩= 108

B7-3 Sightsinging

11
♩ = 96
12
♩ = 138
13
♩ = 96
14
♪ = 144
15
♩ = 92
16
♩ = 80
17
♩ = 120
18
♩. = 80
19
♩ = 92
20
♩ = 76

SERIES B8

DICTATION OF BAR LINES AND METER

In this series there are lessons of two kinds: *bar-line placement*, and *rhythmic dictation of complete phrases*. One of the problems in writing music from dictation is the determination of meter and the place of bar lines. These are the chief problems in this series. The bar line in music usually tells two things: the length of the measure, and the position of the first beat of each measure.

The first beat in the measure, often called the downbeat, is usually the strongest or most emphasized beat. Several characteristics in music can help make a beat sound like a downbeat. A beat tends to sound like a downbeat

1. if it is louder, or accented.
2. if the note beginning on this beat is longer than notes around it.
3. if it occupies the same position in a repeated rhythmic pattern as previous downbeats.
4. if there is a chord change at this point.

It is possible these indications will be contradictory, and some will be more important than others. Generally, when the music contains chords, the chord change is likely to indicate the downbeat even where the other characteristics are contradictory. Where the music is not harmonized, or where there are not important chord changes, strong regular accents are usually more important than long notes in determining the downbeat.

In the example below, the first downbeat is clearly on the first note, which is accented.

In the next example, assuming there are no strong accents, the first downbeat is indicated to be on the third note because it is longer than the notes around it.

Once the first downbeat is determined, the length of measure can be ascertained either by listening for other accented or long notes, or by noting the length of repeated rhythmic patterns. In both examples above, the length of the repeated pattern makes it clear that there is a downbeat every third quarter-note value, and thus the most probable meter is 3/4.

Of course, it is usually not necessary to analyze in this way to find the downbeat. Instead, the above characteristics simply make certain beats sound like downbeats, and, with very little practice, it is possible to detect the position of downbeats without being particularly aware of what makes them sound this way.

Lessons B8-1, B8-2, B8-3, and B8-4. These are lessons in *bar-line placement.* A worksheet and a tape recording are provided for each lesson. In each item on the worksheet, the note values for a melody are written without bar lines. You are to place the bar lines in the appropriate places after you have heard the melody. The answer printed below the sequence of notes shows the proper positions of the bar lines. To do each item, start by shielding the answer. Follow the printed notes while listening to the melody, and try to judge or feel where the downbeats are. Draw a bar line before each downbeat, then uncover the answer and check your response. You may stop the tape recording between items. In these lessons, various characteristics are used to indicate downbeat. In lessons B8-1, B8-2, and B8-3, which have melodies that are not harmonized, you will find the first downbeat indicated either by a strong accent or by a note longer than the others around it. In lesson B8-4, which has harmonized melodies, you may expect chord changes at the downbeats.

Lesson B8-5. This is a lesson in *rhythmic dictation of complete phrases.* A worksheet and a tape recording are provided for this lesson. To do each phrase, start by shielding the printed answer on the right side of the page. For each melody you hear, you are to write the time signature, bar lines, and note values in the space provided. Each melody appears twice on the tape recording. You may stop the tape while writing your answer. After you have responded, slide the shield down and check your response.

B8-1 Bar-line placement

(COPY 1) The following rhythms are in 3/4 meter.

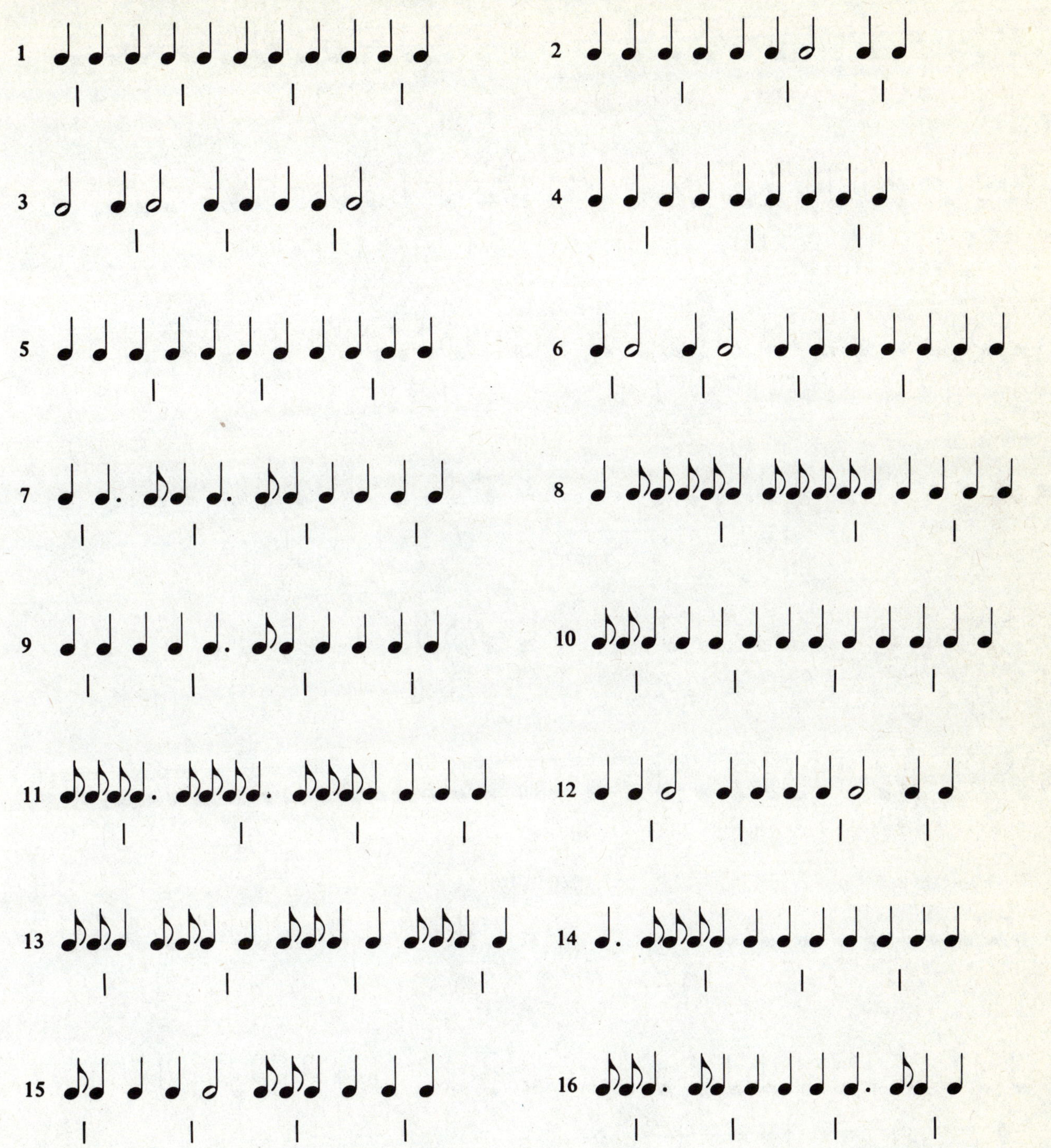

19

20

21

22

23

24

25

26

27

28

29

30

31

32

33

34

35

36

B8-I Bar-line placement

(COPY 2) The following rhythms are in 3/4 meter.

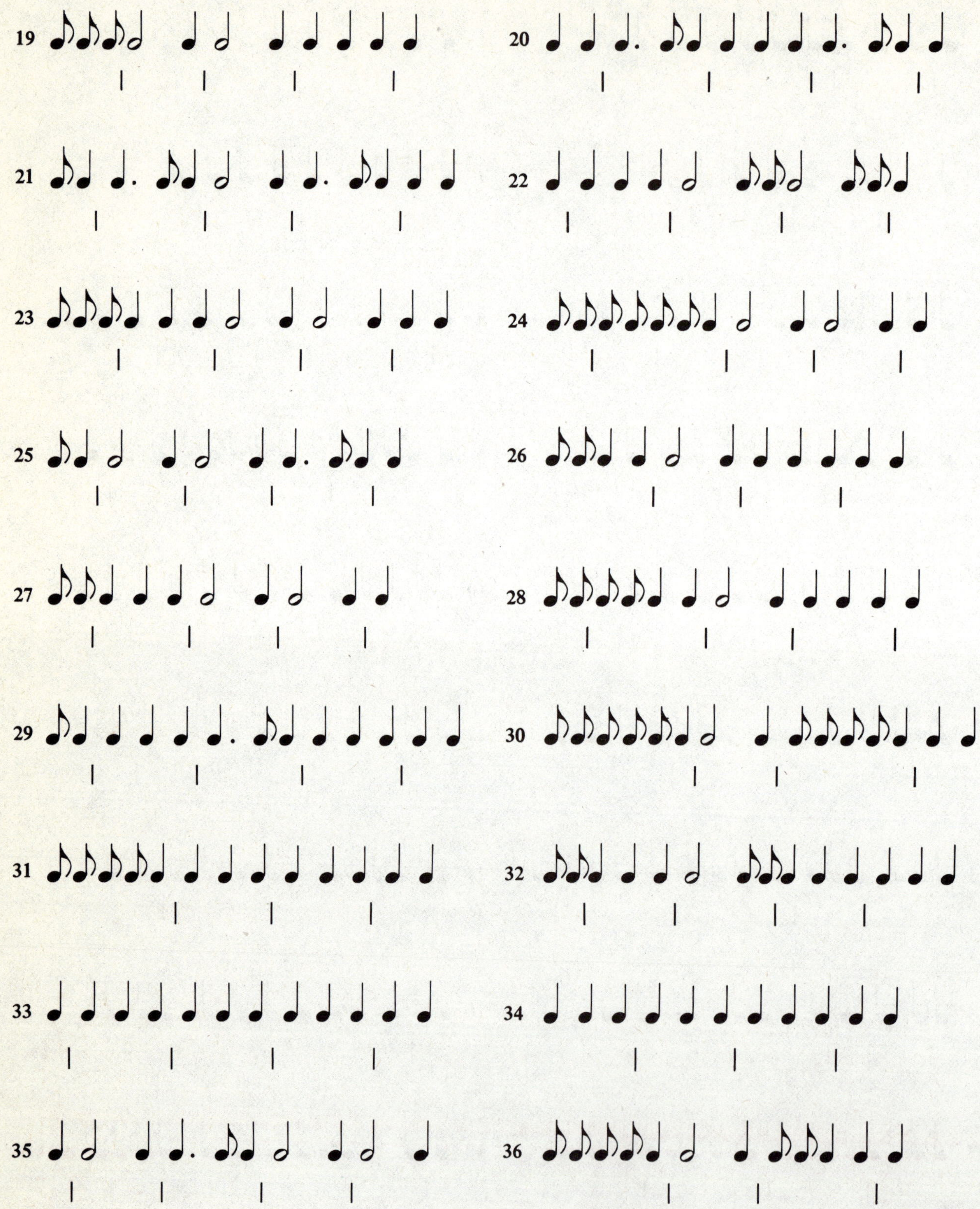

B8-I Bar-line placement

(COPY 3) The following rhythms are in 3/4 meter.

1

2

3

4

5

6

7

8

9

10

11

12

13

14

15

16

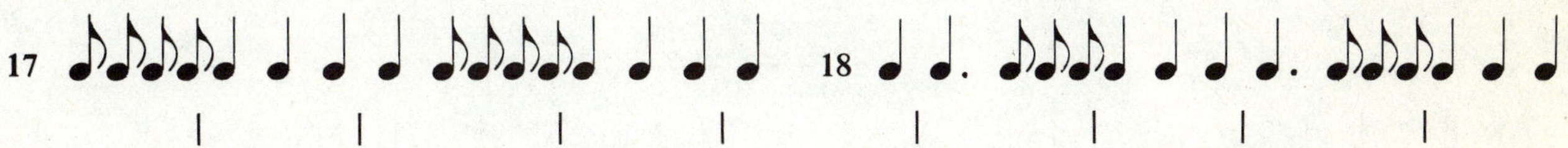

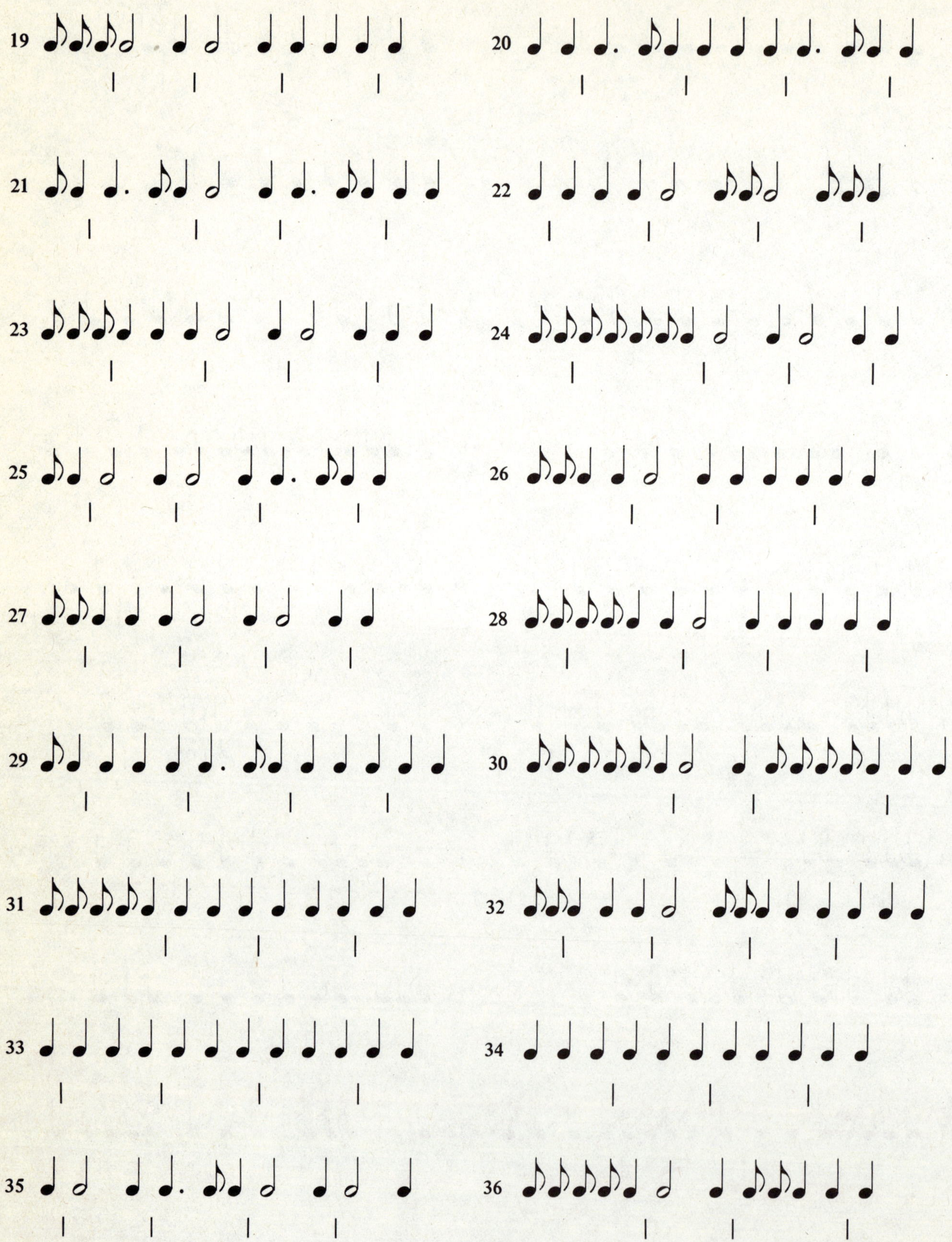
19
20
21
22
23
24
25
26
27
28
29
30
31
32
33
34
35
36

B8-2 Bar-line placement

(COPY 1) The following rhythms are in 4/4 meter.

1

2

3

4

5

6

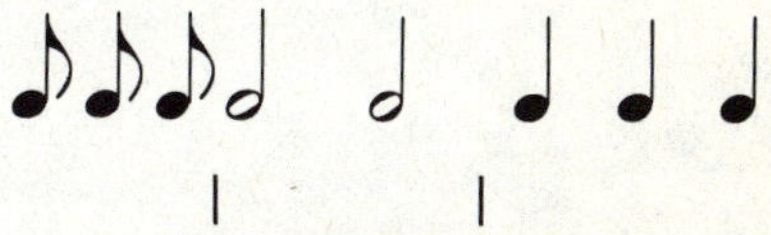

7

8

The following rhythms are in 2/4 meter.

9

10

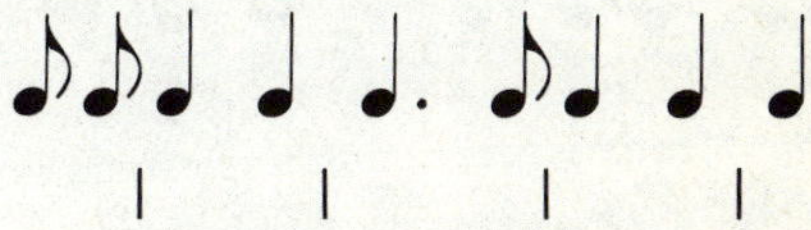

11

12

13

14

15

16

17

18

19

20

21

22

23

24

25

26

27

28

29

30

31

32

33

34

35

36

B8-2 Bar-line placement

(COPY 2) The following rhythms are in 4/4 meter.

1

2

3

4

5

6

7

8

The following rhythms are in 2/4 meter.

9

10

11

12

13

14

15

16

17

18

19

20

21

22

23

24

25

26

27

28

29

30

31

32

33

34

35

36

B8-2 Bar-line placement

(COPY 3) The following rhythms are in 4/4 meter.

1

2

3

4

5

6

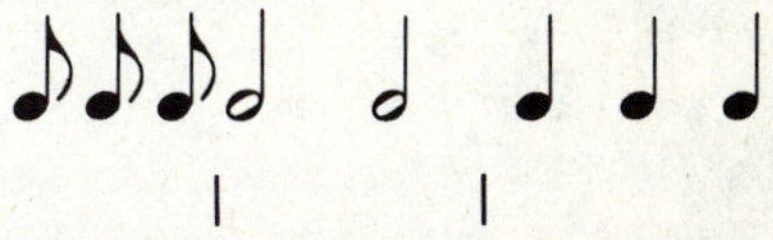

7

8

The following rhythms are in 2/4 meter.

9

10

11

12

13

14

15

16

17

18

19

20

21

22

23

24

25

26

27

28

29

30

31

32

33

34

35

36

B8-3 Bar-line placement

(COPY 1) The following rhythms are in 6/8 meter.

The following rhythms are in 2/4 or 6/8 meter.

19

20

21

22

23

24

25

26

27

28

29

30

31

32

33

34

35

36

B8-3 Bar-line placement

(COPY 2) The following rhythms are in 6/8 meter.

1

2

3

4

5

6

7

8

9

10

11

12

13

14

15

16

17

18

The following rhythms are in 2/4 or 6/8 meter.

19

20

21

22

23

24

25

26

27

28

29

30

31

32

33

34

35

36

B8-3 Bar-line placement

(COPY 3) The following rhythms are in 6/8 meter.

1

2

3

4

5

6

7

8

9

10

11

12

13

14

15

16

17

18

The following rhythms are in 2/4 or 6/8 meter.

19

20

21

22

23

24

25

26

27

28

29

30

31

32

33

34

35

36

B8-4 Bar-line placement

(COPY 1) The following rhythms are in 4/4 or 3/4 meter.

1

2

3

4

5

6

7

8

9

10

11

12

13

14

15

16

17

18

The following rhythms are in 2/4 or 3/4 meter.

19

20

21 

22

23

24

25

26

27

28

29

30

31

32

33

34

35

36

B8-4 Bar-line placement

(COPY 2) The following rhythms are in 4/4 or3/4 meter.

1 

2

3 

4 

5 

6 

7 

8 

9 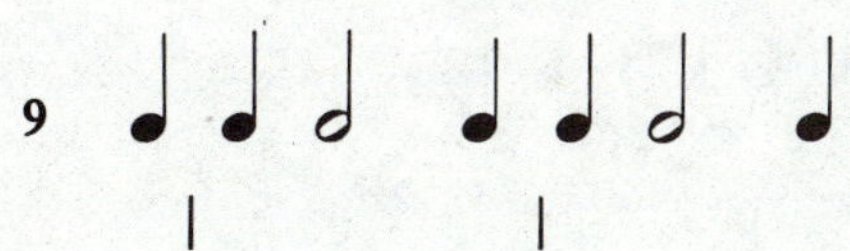

10 

11

12

13

14

15

16

17

18

The following rhythms are in 2/4 or 3/4 meter.

19 

20

21

22

23

24

25

26

27

28

29

30

31

32

33

34

35

36

B8-4 Bar-line placement

(COPY 3) The following rhythms are in 4/4 or3/4 meter.

1 

2

3 

4 

5 

6

7 

8 

9

10

11

12

13

14

15

16

17

18

The following rhythms are in 2/4 or 3/4 meter.

19 

20

21

22

23

24

25

26

27

28

29

30

31

32

33

34

35

36

B8-5 Rhythmic dictation of complete phrases

(COPY 1) The following rhythms are in 3/4 or 4/4 meter.

1

2

3

4

5

6

7

8

9

The following rhythms are in 6/8 or 2/4 meter.

10

11

12

13

14

15

16

17

18

The following rhythms are in 2/4 or 3/4 meter.

19

20

21

22

23

24

B8-5 Rhythmic dictation of complete phrases

(COPY 2) The following rhythms are in 3/4 or 4/4 meter.

1

2

3

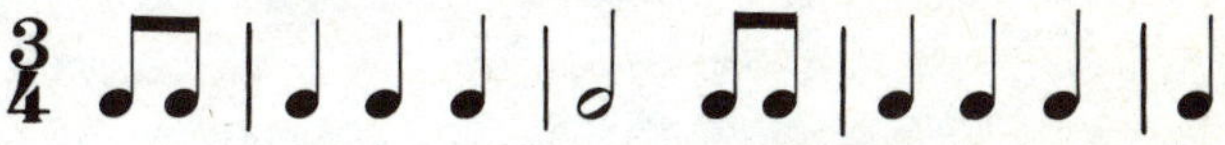

4

5

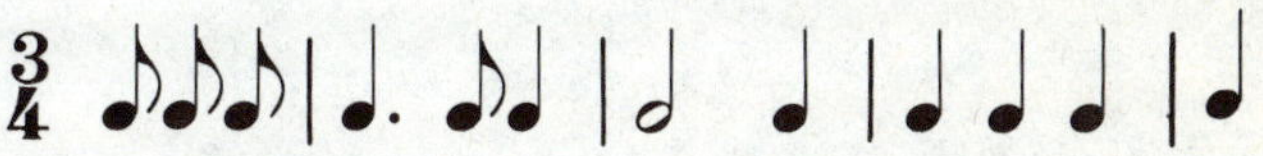

6

7

8

9

The following rhythms are in 6/8 or 2/4 meter.

10

11

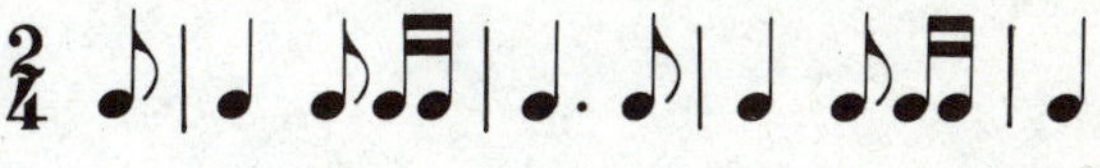

12

13

14

15

16

17

18

The following rhythms are in 2/4 or 3/4 meter.

19

20

21

22

23

24

B8-5 Rhythmic dictation of complete phrases

(COPY 3) The following rhythms are in 3/4 or 4/4 meter.

1 3/4

2 4/4

3 3/4

4 4/4

5 3/4

6 4/4

7 3/4

8 4/4

9 3/4

The following rhythms are in 6/8 or 2/4 meter.

10 6/8

11 2/4

12 6/8

13

14

15

16

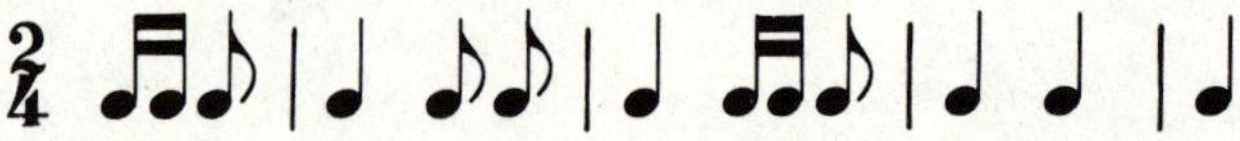

17

18

The following rhythms are in 2/4 or 3/4 meter.

19

20

21

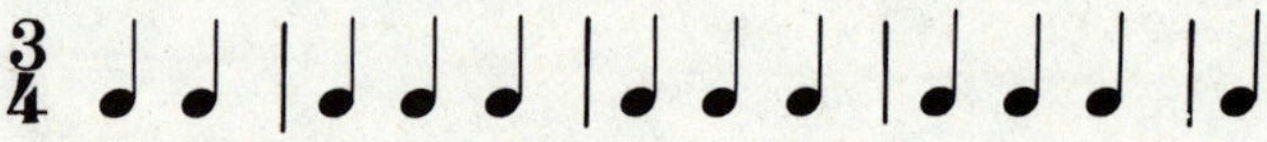

22

23

24

SERIES B9

MELODIC DICTATION OF COMPLETE PHRASES

The purpose of this series is to develop the ability to notate the pitches and rhythm of complete phrases you hear. An answer sheet and a tape recording are provided for each lesson. You must use your own manuscript paper for your answers.

To do each lesson, first shield the long correct answer on the page, leaving revealed only the starting note and the two time signatures on the left side. Start the tape and listen to the melody. It will be performed twice. Then stop the tape, select one of the two time signatures and write the melody. If necessary, you can rewind the tape for further hearings. After you have written out a melody, look at the answer sheet to check your answer, and go on to the next melody.

B9-I Melodic dictation

B9-2 Melodic dictation

B9-3 Melodic dictation

B9-4 Melodic dictation

B9-5 Melodic dictation

SERIES B10

SIGHTSINGING OF SKIPS AND ACCIDENTALS

The purpose of this series is to develop the ability to sightsing melodies containing wide skips and accidentals. The melodies are rhythmically simple so you can concentrate on accidentals and skips. A musical score and tape recording are provided for each lesson.

The procedure for this series is the same as for Series B2. Start the tape and you will hear a metronome tempo and the starting tone for the first melody. After the starting tone, sing the melody with the metronome and listen for the recorded correct melody. Immediately sing the second melody, and so on with each melody.

B10-1 Sightsinging

B10-2 Sightsinging

B10-3 Sightsinging

B10-1 Lesson supplements

B10-3 Lesson supplements

SERIES B11

MELODIC DICTATION OF SKIPS AND ACCIDENTALS

The purpose of this series is to develop the ability to write melodies you hear containing accidentals and wide skips. The procedure is the same as for Series B3. A printed worksheet and tape recording are provided for each lesson. The melodies are rhythmically simple so you can concentrate on accidentals and skips.

BII-1 **Melodic dictation**
(COPY 1)

BII-I Melodic dictation

(COPY 2)

BII-I Melodic dictation

(COPY 3)

BII-2 Melodic dictation

(COPY 1)

BII-2 Melodic dictation
(COPY 2)

BII-2 Melodic dictation
(COPY 3)

BII-3 Melodic dictation
(COPY 1)

BII-3 Melodic dictation

(COPY 2)

BII-3 Melodic dictation
(COPY 3)

SERIES B12

SIGHTSINGING OF MODULATIONS

The purpose of this series is to develop the ability to sightsing melodies containing modulations. A printed score and tape recording are provided for each lesson. The melodies are of intermediate length and fairly simple except for the modulations.

The procedure is the same as for other sightsinging lessons. The starting tone is given for only the first melody. The starting tone for the others can be judged from the pitches of the preceding melody.

B12-1 Sightsinging

B12-2 Sightsinging

B12-3 Sightsinging

B12-1 Lesson supplements

B12-2 Lesson supplements

B12-3 Lesson supplements

SERIES B13

ADVANCED SIGHTSINGING

The lessons of this series contain short melodies that are of more advanced difficulty both in pitch and rhythm. The procedure is the same as for other sightsinging lessons.

The starting tone is provided for only the first melody. The starting tone for the others can be judged from the pitches of the preceding melody.

B13-1 Sightsinging

B13-2 Sightsinging

3
3

B13-3 Sightsinging

B13-4 Sightsinging

3
3

B13-5 Sightsinging

B13-6 Sightsinging

B13-7 Sightsinging

B13-8 Sightsinging

B13-9 Sightsinging

B13-1 Lesson supplements

B13-2 Lesson supplements

B13-3 Lesson supplements

B13-4 Lesson supplements

B13-5 Lesson supplements

B13-6 Lesson supplements

1

2

3

4

5

6

B13-7 Lesson supplements

B13-8 Lesson supplements

B13-9 Lesson supplements

SERIES B14

ADVANCED MELODIC DICTATION

The lessons of this series contain short melodies that are of more advanced difficulty both in pitch and rhythm. The procedure is the same as in other dictation lessons.

B14-1 Melodic dictation
(COPY 1)

3
3

B14-1 Melodic dictation
(COPY 2)

3
3

B14-1 Melodic dictation

(COPY 3)

B14-2 Melodic dictation
(COPY 1)

B14-2 Melodic dictation

(COPY 2)

B14-2 Melodic dictation
(COPY 3)

B14-3 Melodic dictation

(COPY 1)

B14-3 Melodic dictation

(COPY 2)

B14-3 Melodic dictation
(COPY 3)

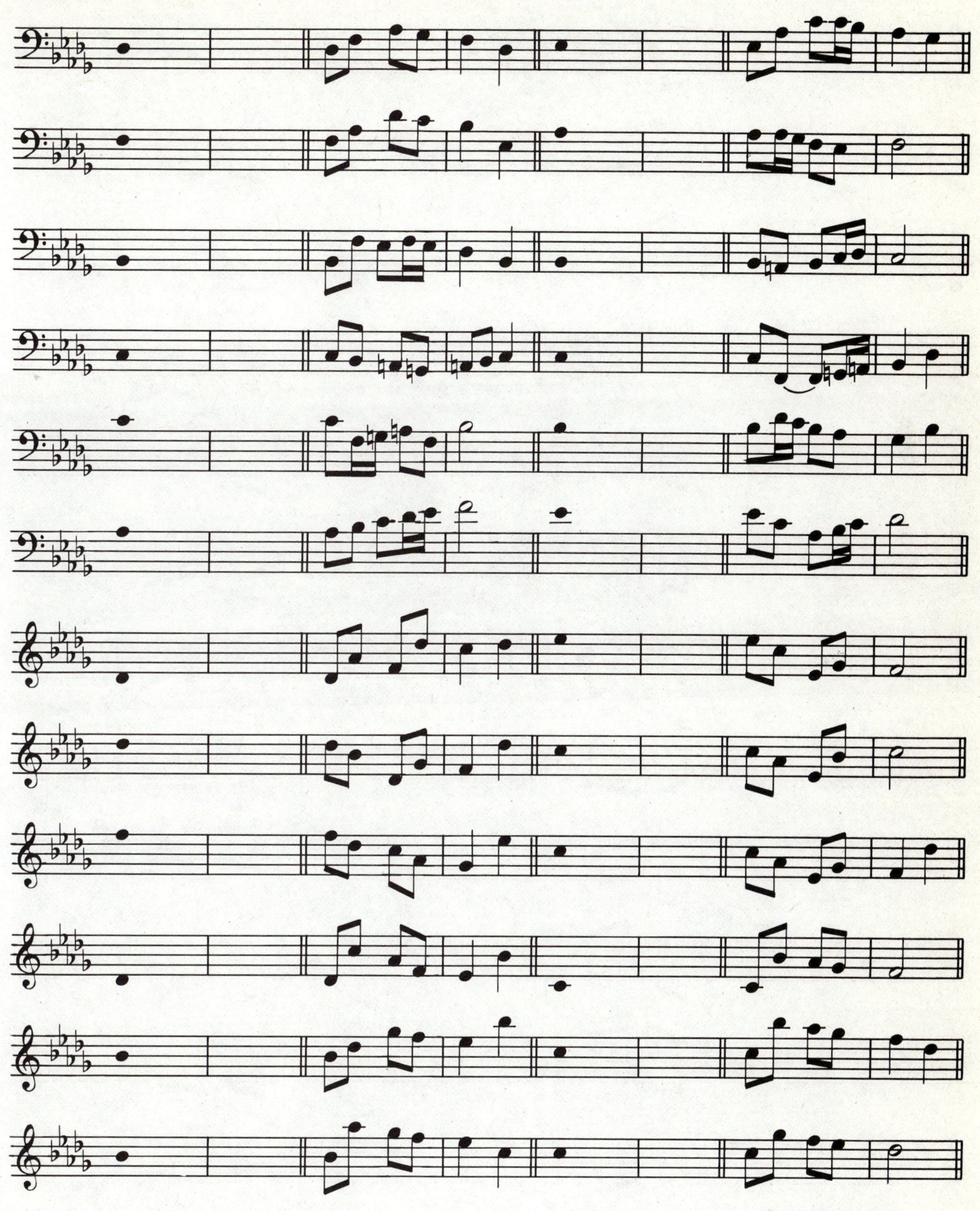

B14-4 Melodic dictation

(COPY 1)

B14-4 Melodic dictation

(COPY 2)

B14-4 Melodic dictation

(COPY 3)

B14-5 Melodic dictation

(COPY 1)

B14-5 Melodic dictation
(COPY 2)

B14-5 Melodic dictation
(COPY 3)

B14-6 Melodic dictation

(COPY 1)

B14-6 Melodic dictation
(COPY 2)

B14-6 Melodic dictation

(COPY 3)

SERIES B15

SIGHTSINGING OF COMPLETE PHRASES WITH MODULATIONS

The purpose of this series is to develop the ability to sightsing long melodies with modulations. A printed score and tape recording are provided for each lesson.

Each melody consists of a complete line. To do a lesson, start the tape to hear the tempo and starting tone. Then stop the tape and sing the complete melody. Again start the tape and you will hear only the part of the melody that appears after the sign 𝄋. You should sing the complete melody in order to experience the modulation, but should judge the correctness of your response only with reference to the last part of the melody. You will hear the starting tone for only the first melody. The starting tone for the others can be judged from the pitches of the preceding melody.

B15-1 Sightsinging

B15-2 Sightsinging

B15-3 Sightsinging

SERIES B16

MELODIC DICTATION OF COMPLETE PHRASES WITH MODULATIONS

The purpose of this series is to develop the ability to write complete melodies with modulations that you hear. An answer sheet and tape recording are provided for each lesson. You must use your own manuscript paper for your answers.

To do each lesson, first shield the long correct answers on the page leaving revealed only the starting note and the two time signatures on the left. Start the tape and listen to the melody. It will be performed twice. Then stop the tape, select one of the two time signatures, and write the melody. Use the signature of the key in which the melody begins, and appropriate accidentals where modulations occur. If necessary, you can rewind the tape for further hearings. After you have written out a melody, look at the answer sheet to check your answer, and go on to the next melody.

B16-1 Melodic dictation

B16-2 Melodic dictation

B16-3 Melodic dictation

B16-4 Melodic dictation

B16-5 Melodic dictation

SERIES B17

SIGHTSINGING OF COMPLETE PHRASES

This series is similar to Series B9, except the melodies here are more complex. The procedure is the same.

Each melody consists of an entire line. Before starting each melody, observe the metronome marking and the note value, which will receive one beat. Observe the key signature to determine the key, and the degree of the key on which the melody begins. For those melodies that do not begin on the tonic, you may find it helpful to sing scalewise from the starting note to the tonic in order to help establish the key in your mind.

To do the lesson, start the tape recording. You will hear the metronome tempo and the pitch of the first melody. Stop the tape after hearing this, and sing the first melody. Start the tape again to hear the melody correctly performed. You will then hear the tempo and the starting tone for the next melody.

B17-1 Sightsinging

11
= 80
12
= 80
13
= 80
14
= 126
15
= 88
16
= 126
17
= 60
18
= 76
19
= 88
20
= 92

B17-2 Sightsinging

11
♩ = 116
12
♩ = 88
13
𝅗𝅥 = 92
14
♩. = 60
15
♩ = 108
16
♩ = 92
17
♩ = 76
18
♩ = 116
19
♩ = 76
20
𝅗𝅥 = 84

B17-3 Sightsinging

11
♩ = 76
12
♩ = 100
13
♪ = 108
14
𝅗𝅥 = 96
15
♩ = 100
16
♪ = 72
17
♩ = 116
18
♪ = 126
19
♩ = 88
20
♩ = 108